High Shelf

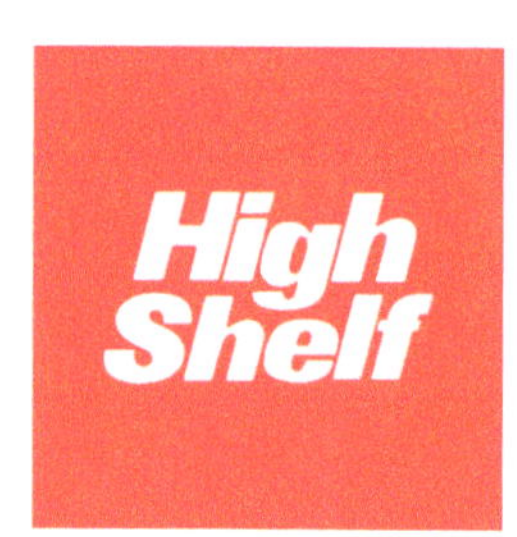

High Shelf XXV. December 2020.
Portland, Oregon.
Copyright 2020, High Shelf Press

ISBN: 978-1-952869-21-1

Cover Image by Stuart Terman
Design and Layout by C. M. Tollefson
Editing by David Seung & C. M. Tollefson

With special thanks to:
Kelsey Beck Kuther, Megan Kim, & River Elizabeth Hall.

High Shelf XXV

December 2020

"this is the language
in which you build
a world you already know..."
                    Anna Winham

"... your dreams are

needy: they come uninvited, waking me..."
Silja Cheong

Table Of Contents

Pinning Down the Crossroads

Caroline Rowe

The blues, the soul's
mange,
moon bald,
spleen hued,
cries answered
by cries.
The blues skies
foreshadow insanity,
baptize,
make us hungry,
crumple the colorless
parchments of transcendence,
keep our rags
wet.
Clarksdale, Mississippi,
endless farmland, then
a city,
mostly abandoned
where Son House
got the death letter;
Rev. Son House, so fearing
God, could not lie
but in each anthem
cried and sputtered
like a disorder
his only truth:
It's so hard to love someone
who don't love you.
Sam Cooke, milky
and murdered
first rooted his fine feet
in this silver gospel soil.
Here, the downtown
he was told,
don't hang around

while Howlin' Wolf
in harrowing hollers,
the haggard hound's bays,
exhaled his heart
in a harmonica
and huffed the red pulp.
John Lee Hooker,
his eyes weepy, frightening
with clit-rubbing guitar,
I'm mad. I'm bad this morning.
Robert Johnson's sinister stare
makes the blood oath
for your momentary psyche.
Robert Johnson, legend has it,
at the Clarksdale crossroads
traded his salvation
to moan.
It's argued though
the real crossroads
is down in Rosedale,
Highway 1 and Highway 8,
with no cheesy sign
but flanked by an elementary school
and a defunct café.
They say the devil
 would not stray
so far from the river,
where our home New Orleans voodoo
sperms its cross-current way,
against the south bound
thundering mud
to sire from the delta's womb
the blues, unhallowed
and adversarial.
We drive down
to Rosedale, through the visionary cold,
the cotton dregs like snow
on the shoulder of the road.
Crawling king snake,
low down dance of fog.
We arrive at the coordinates,
so utterly
anonymous, strewn
with empty bottles
of gas station liquor.

Wet grass. Car horns.
In our city shoes, we cross,
pace and finally foot
our way in the mouth
of the mousetrap
of the wail
of the whip
of the rip
of the true
your-love-is-dead
woah-stop-your-train
old-evil-spirit
Delta blues.

Alone in the Sky

Abe Winterscheidt

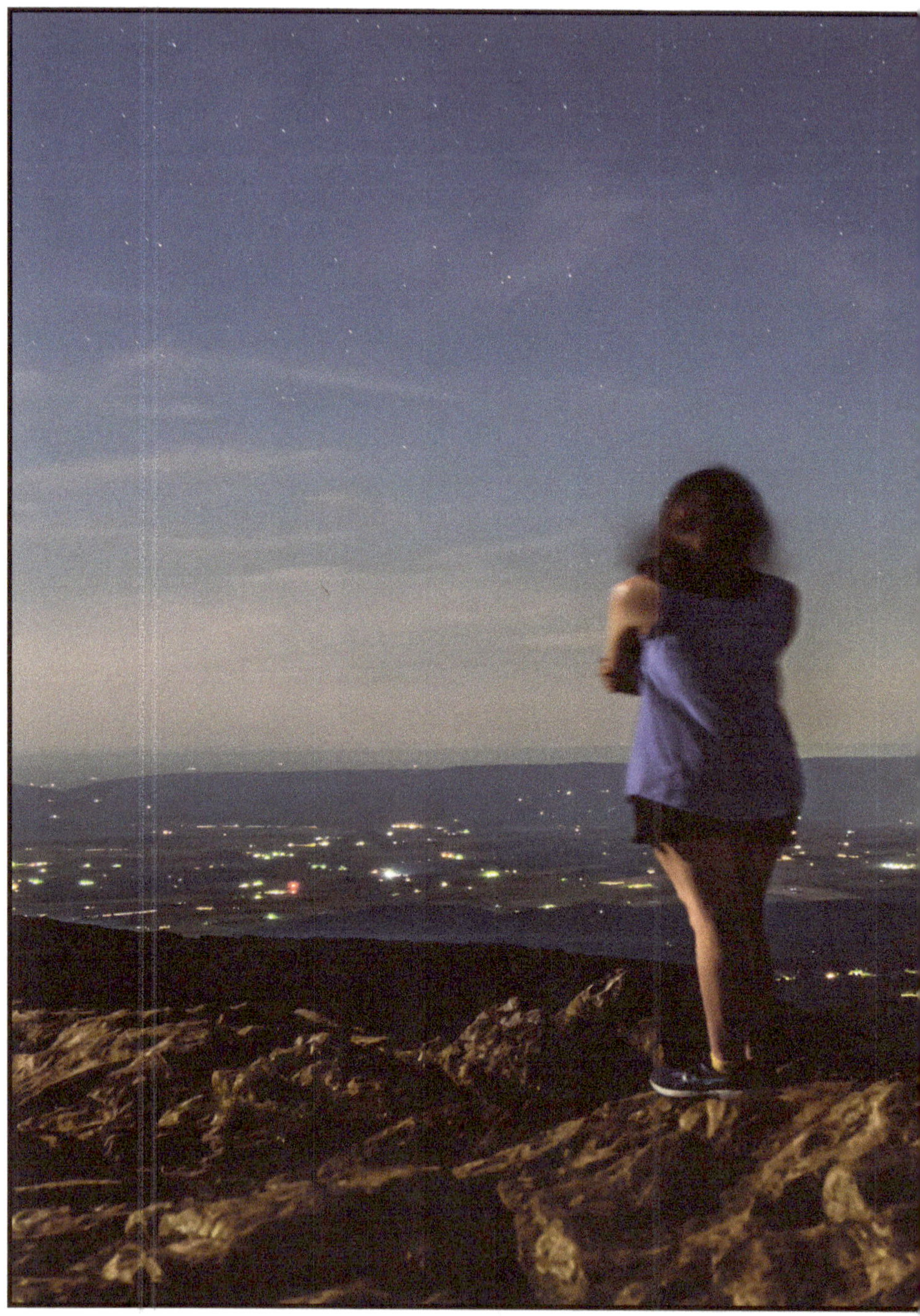

Nocturne with Sudden Americana

James King

Post-July 4th, 2020

I have to wonder

every night at nine   the woods becomes a drum
the sound and not the fire   of fireworks—
yes   *every summer night*   since the winter I was born
and that was a while ago—

some nights I slide out under a porchlight   I drink and I listen
usually across the street   there is a bonfire
the accompanying rings   of orange-painted people
and sometimes they jam a stick   through a dead pig—
there is also   I might add   the distant pretense
of light beer —

look this is a town of old houses and dying white men
which is to say   I let them have their fun
and I have learned to sleep through the thunder   but
sometimes I'm curious   if they will light a rocket
while I am watching
I'm curious to know who it is they think they've beaten—   these people
in baseball caps   in their Friday-night circles—
I have to admit   I want to know their reason
for declaring victory

Hunting.

Jason R. Montgomery

The first time I returned to you
With the meat of a rattlesnake
You beat me.

You sent me out into the desert
With rifle, shovel and hoe.

Across creek, dust and sun,
Told to avoid the mountain,
To stray not too far,
Or exist as an alien,
Illegal
In a place exactly like the one I left.

You sent me out
With message, and motive.

Across the highway of black asphalt and yellow paint
And the sun,
And the sun,
And the sun,

Told to look first with my ears,
To hear next with my eyes,
And fight
As situation deemed necessary.

And the serpent lay in the sun,
And in the sun,
In the sun,
In the sun,
In instinct of care abandoned.

If brush and weeds provided cover,
Cracked earth and stone
An exit,
The ability to walk endlessly avoiding the mountain
At the end of the world.

But rather to both paths end at my ignorance
And inability to let be be.

You will never get this,
But I will still imagine you
Wandering the streets with
Pastels,
Watercolors,
Streams,
Dreams,
And hope for returning to a better land.

HAD THEY KNOWN BETTER THEY WOULD HAVE DONE BETTER

Ninel Nekay

As an adult
who is unavoidably someone
else's child

I conclude, crazy is betrayal
grown up.

It is the soreness that derives from our historic indebtedness
to ancient nouns that owe us
apologies.

Mixed Media: Matter / Seers / Made with American Cotton I / Flow

Lea Wülferth

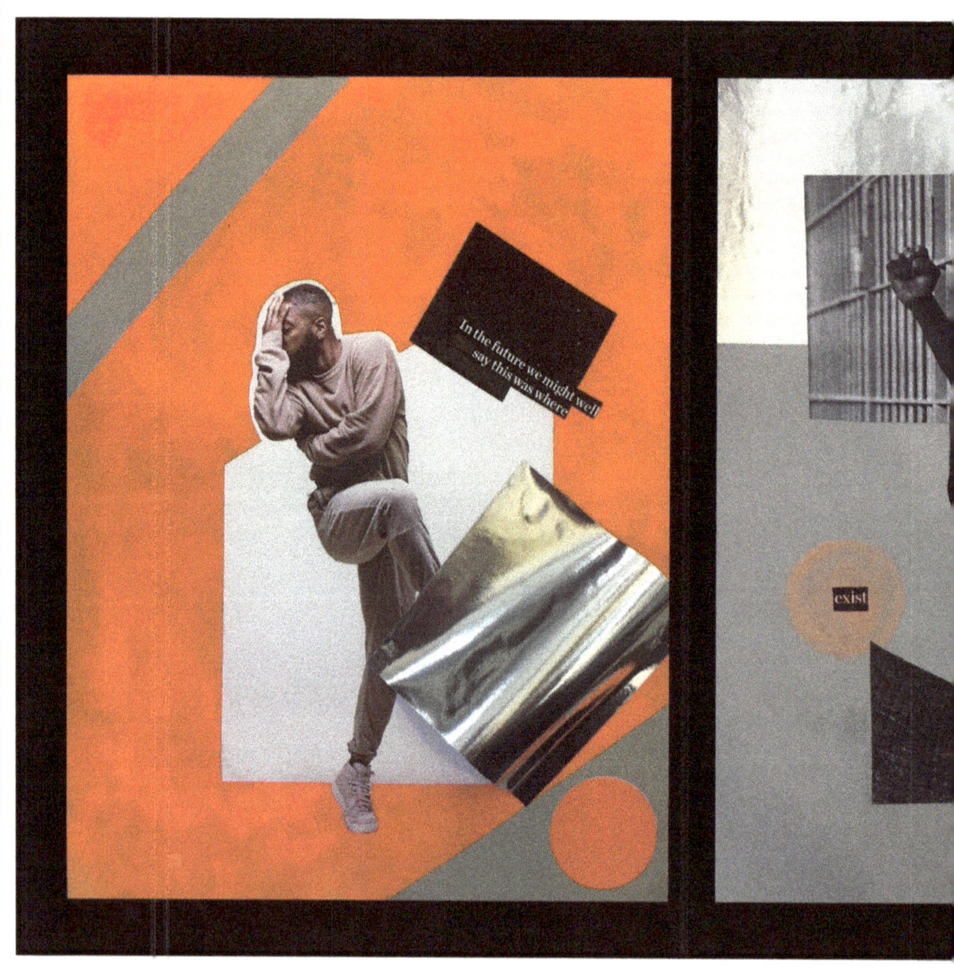

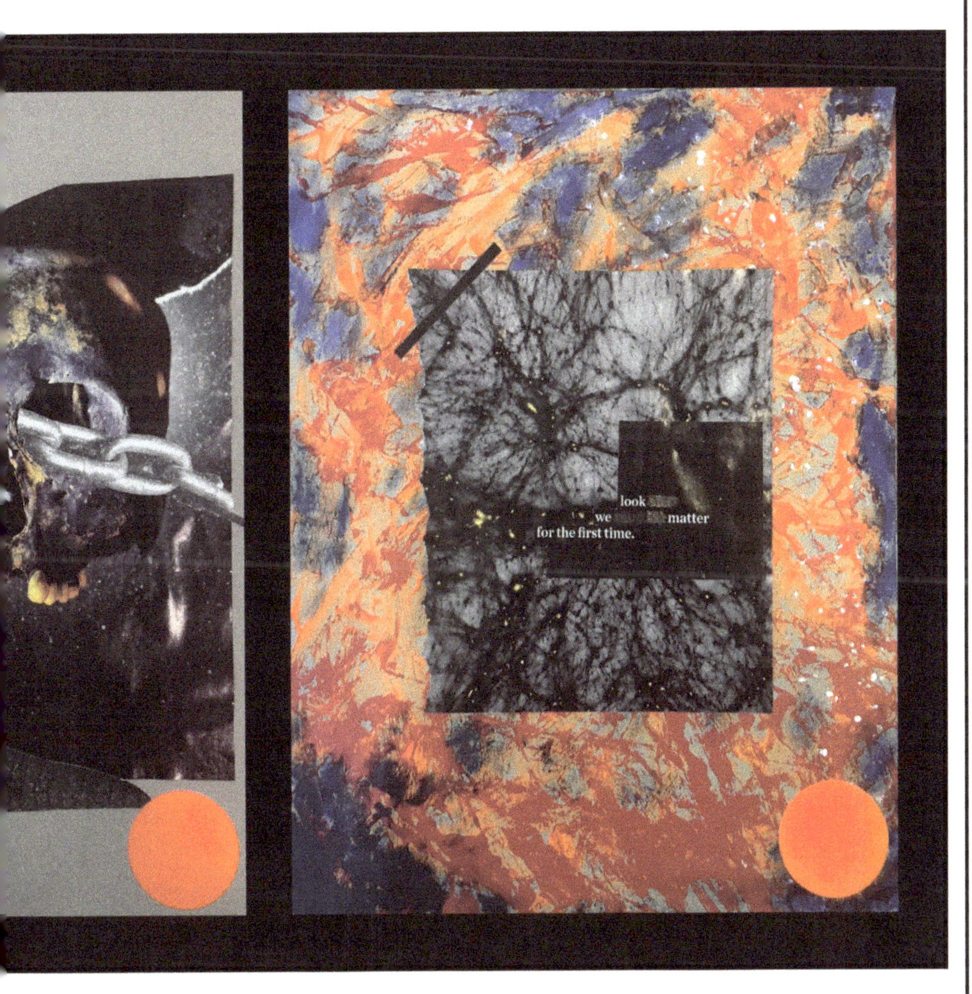
look
we   matter
for the first time.

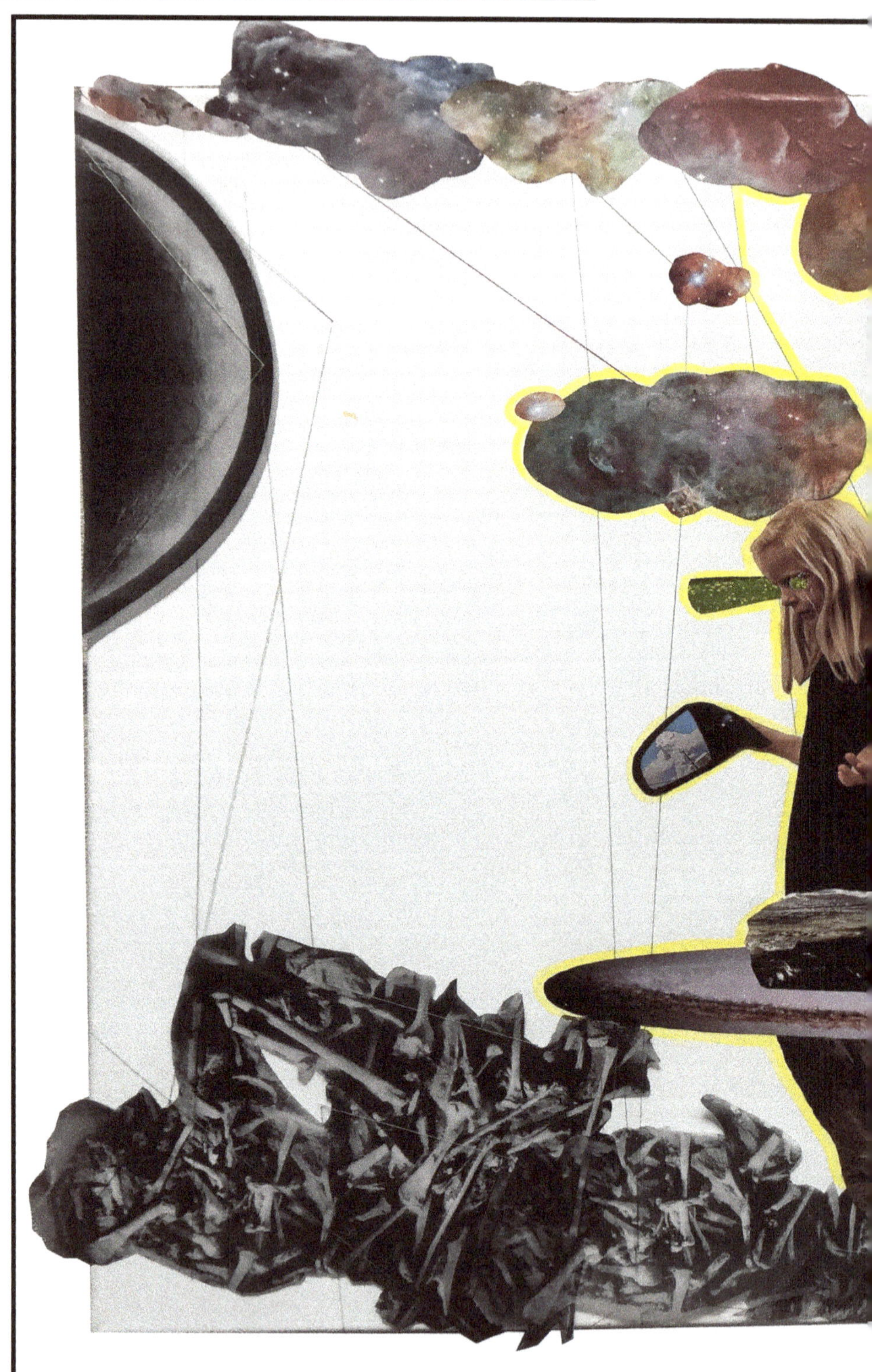

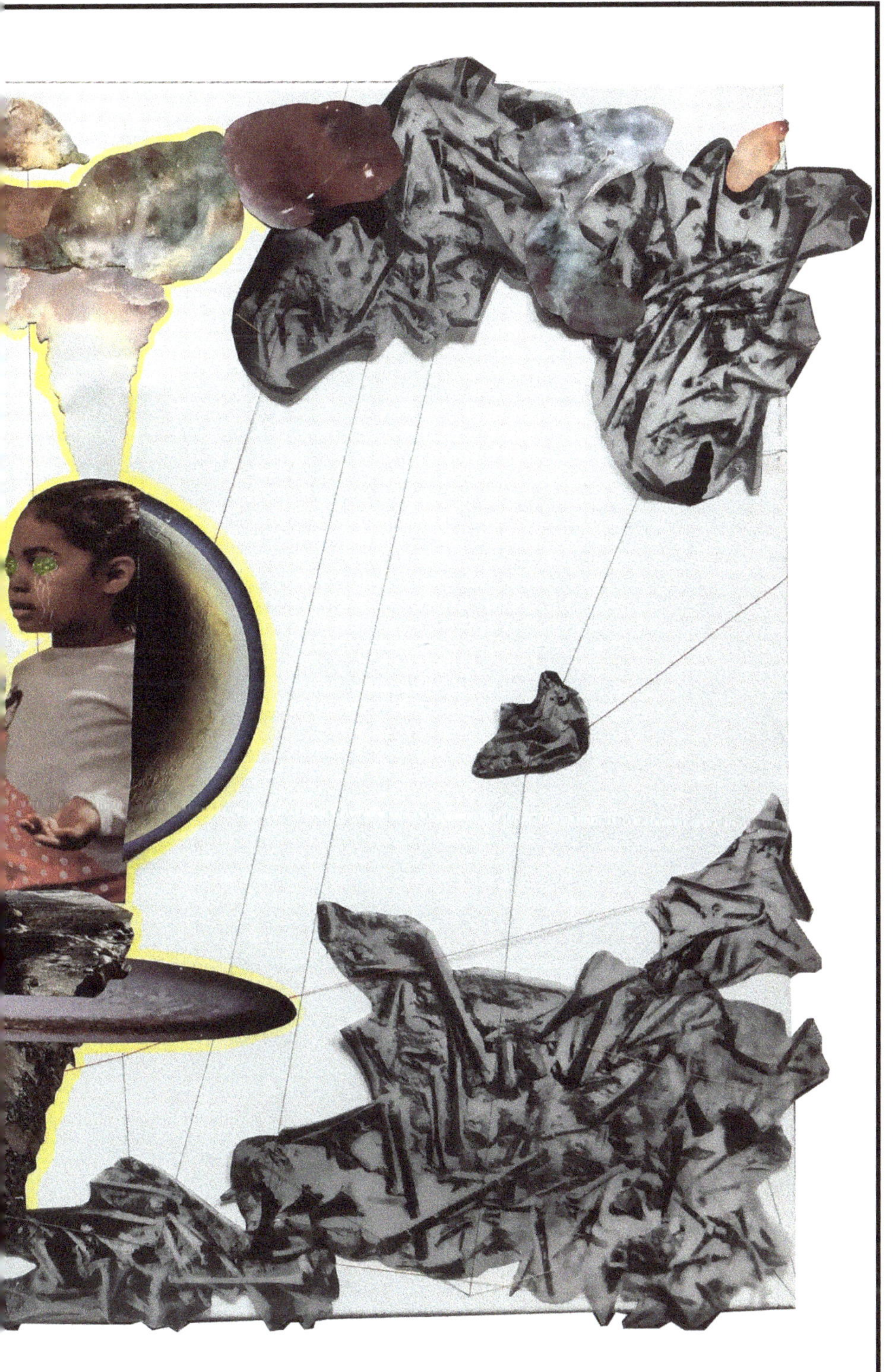

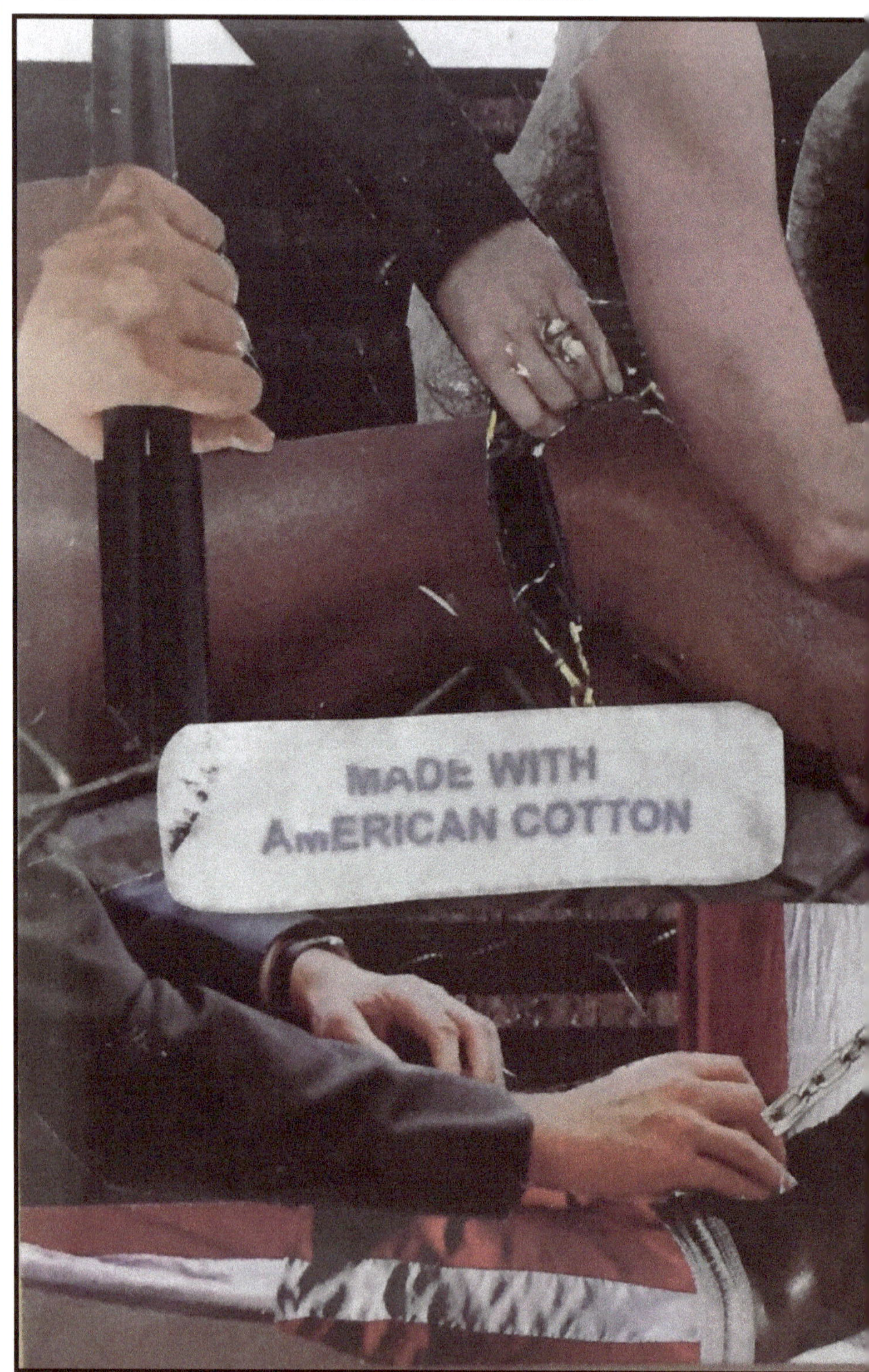

MADE WITH
AmERICAN COTTON

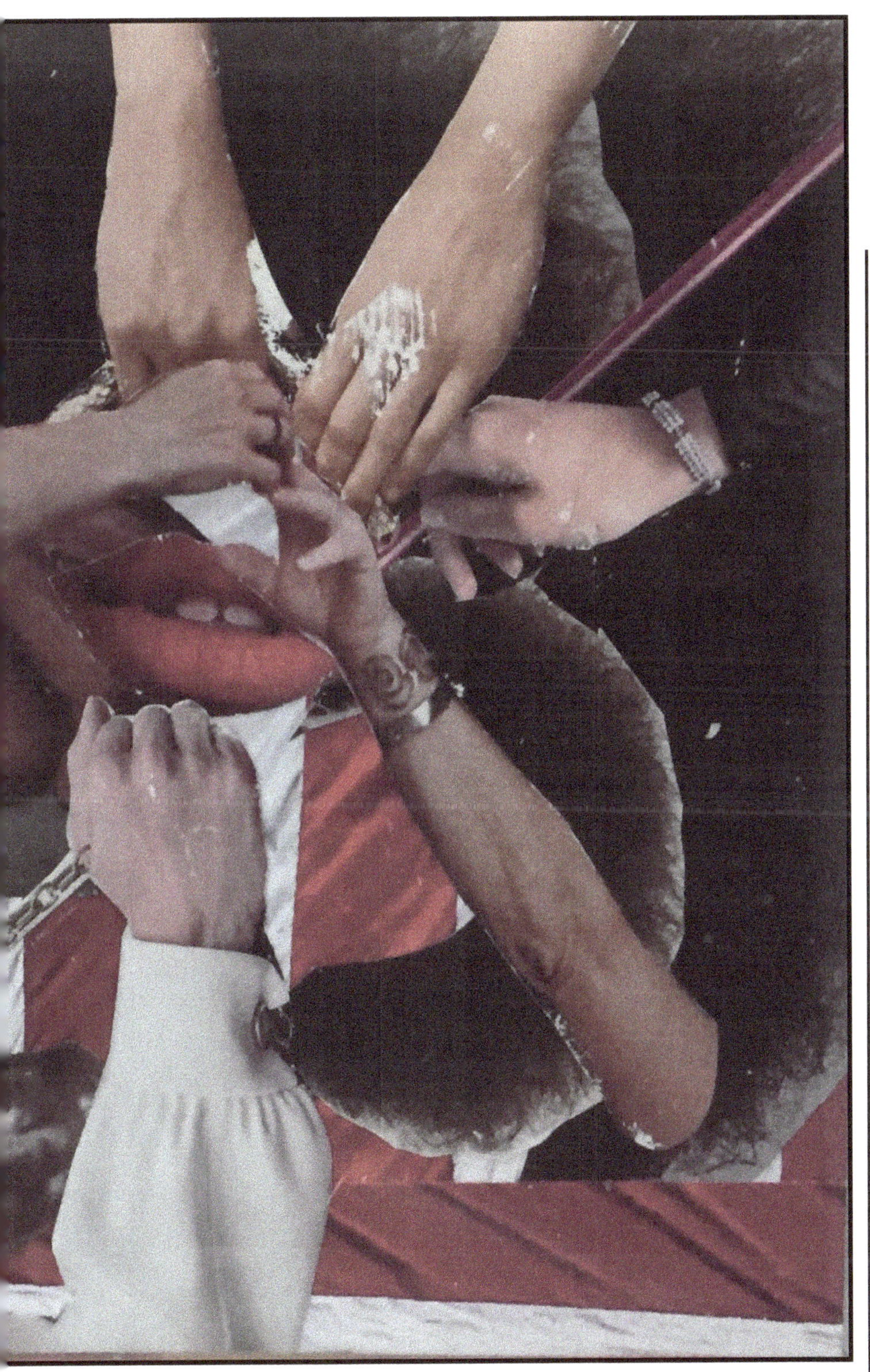

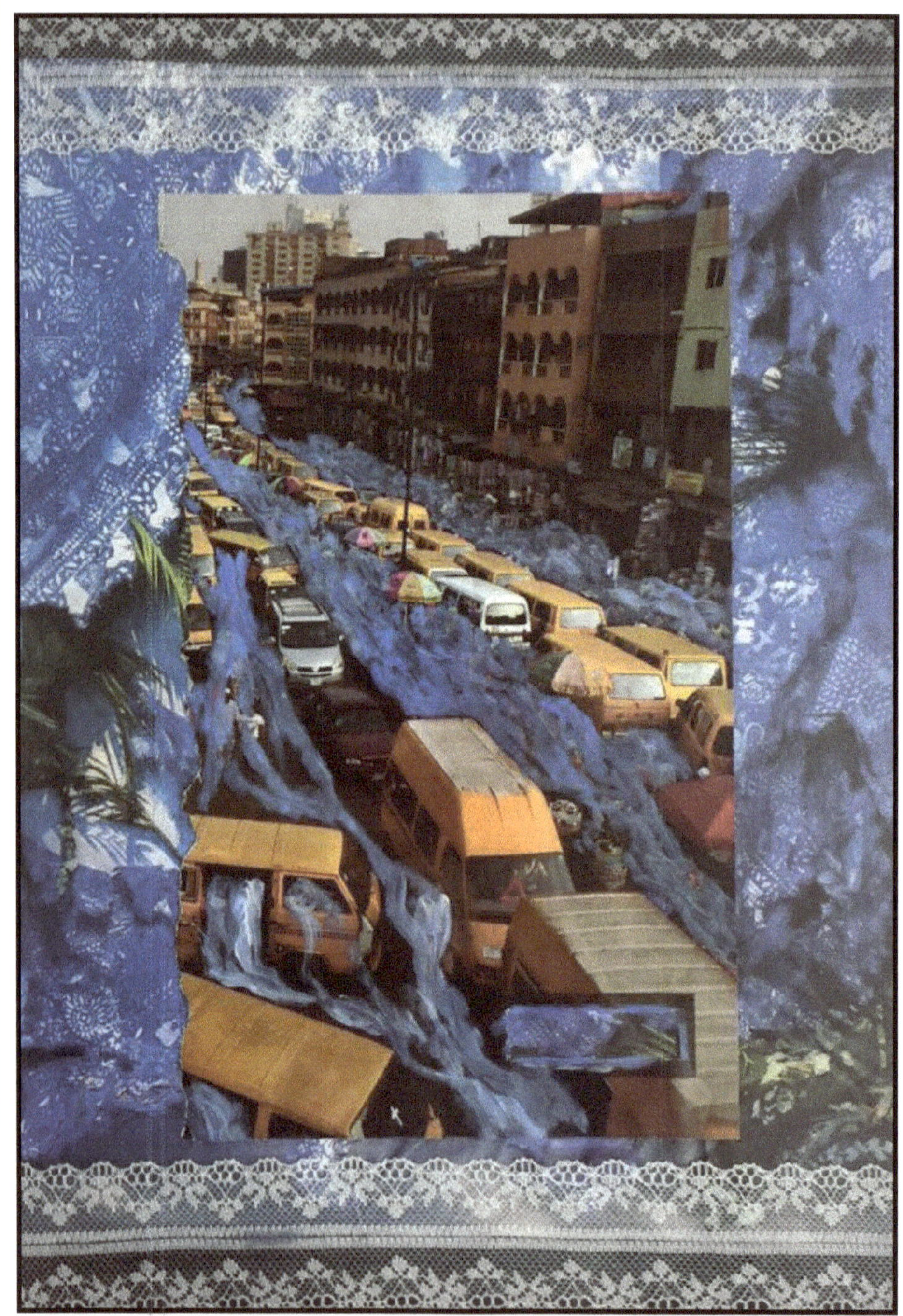

O.

Silja Cheong

what if. what if you find your way

in (again), what if you come

telling me

I want to see

God, which one? your dreams are

needy: they come uninvited, waking me

up at night, the sheets

reek of uncertainties, raw skin. words fall

off of you so easily, what if

I knew that you would not love me

If I made any sense to you? I breathe, and the air

takes your shape.

Love grass

Ma. Antonette Lofamia

Mursikos, my grandmother would say,
her linguistic stubbornness waving
the white church clothes in my face,
must not cling to the skirts of this dress.
Don't embarrass me in front of Padre.

Amorseko.

My grandmother, who would spell
Filipino words in Spanish, was not
unaware of this grass's etymology:
from the Spanish, amor-seco,

dry love.

In her intimacy and seriousness,
my grandmother had kept hold of our lands,
kept hold of our name, kept hold of this, too:
it is not love what comes dry. Mursikos.

Amor-

seco. Grandmother would refuse the word
the same way she refused the merry dance
of her husband's gun. It is not love what comes
dry. Mursikos, grandmother would say instead,

bruises.

I am now in the train staring at the mursikos
stuck on the bottoms of my second-hand jeans,
my entire body feeling the rightness of it there.
Amorseko. There is no shame in this.
Amor has nuances and some are exactly this.

Marvelous Voyage

Joy Kloman

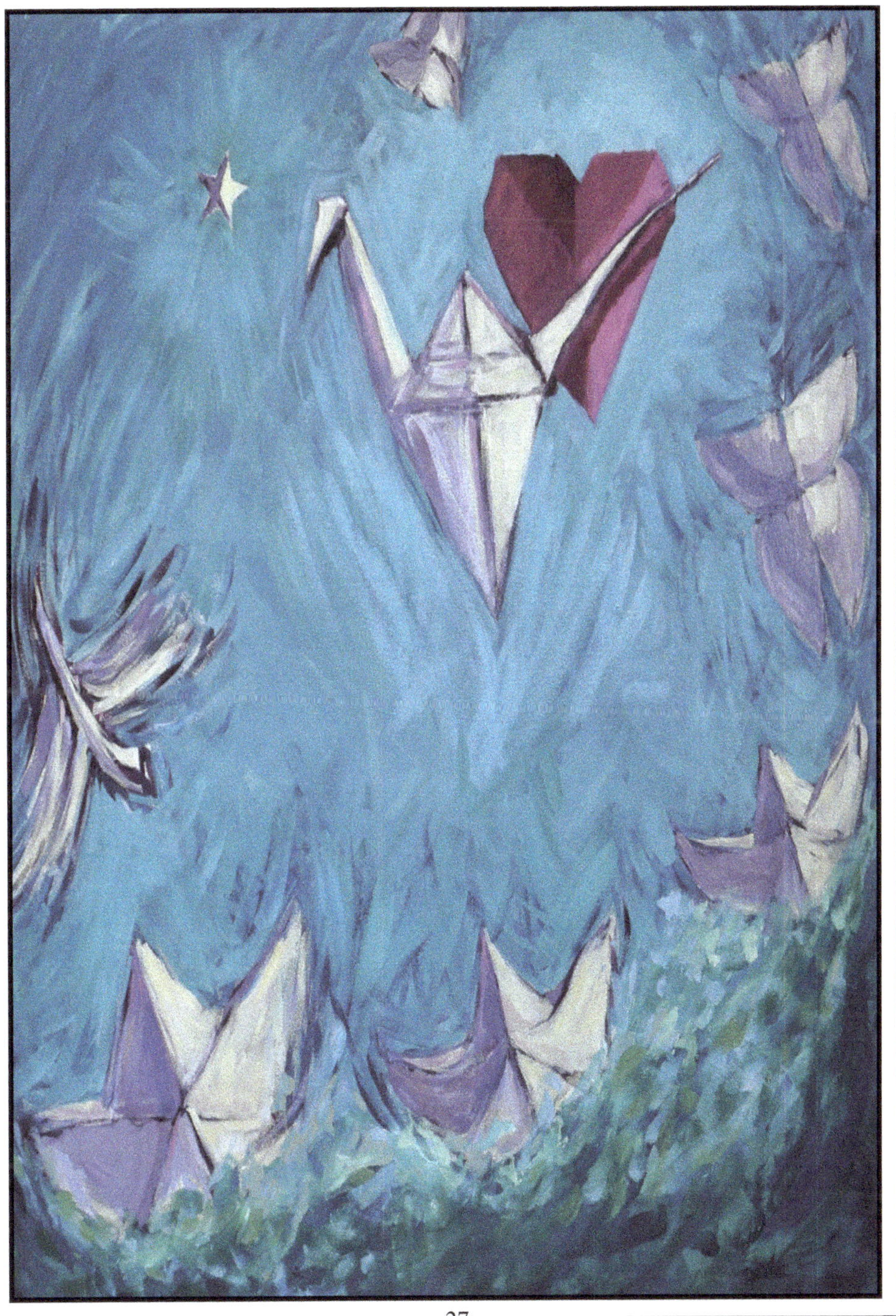

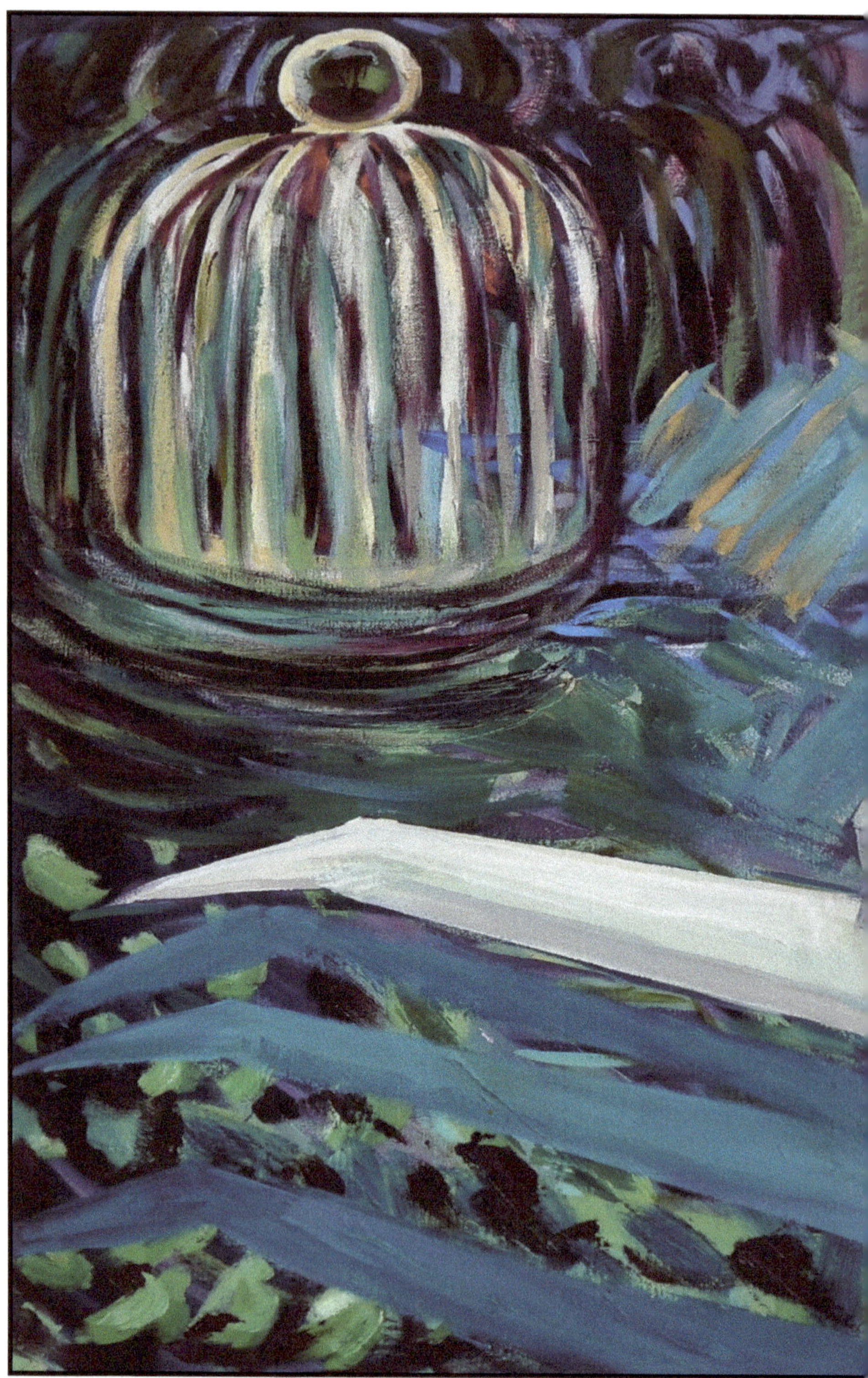

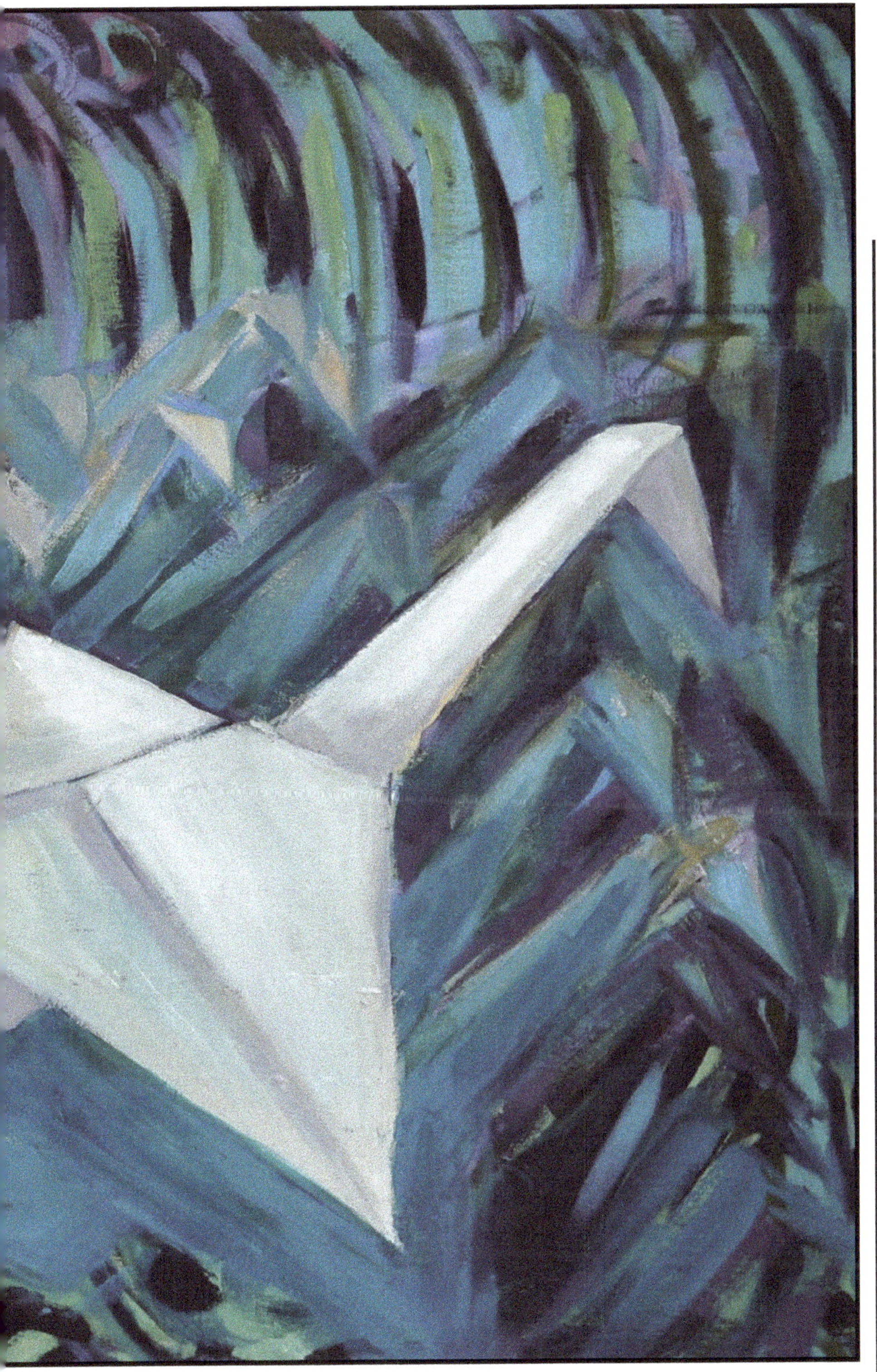

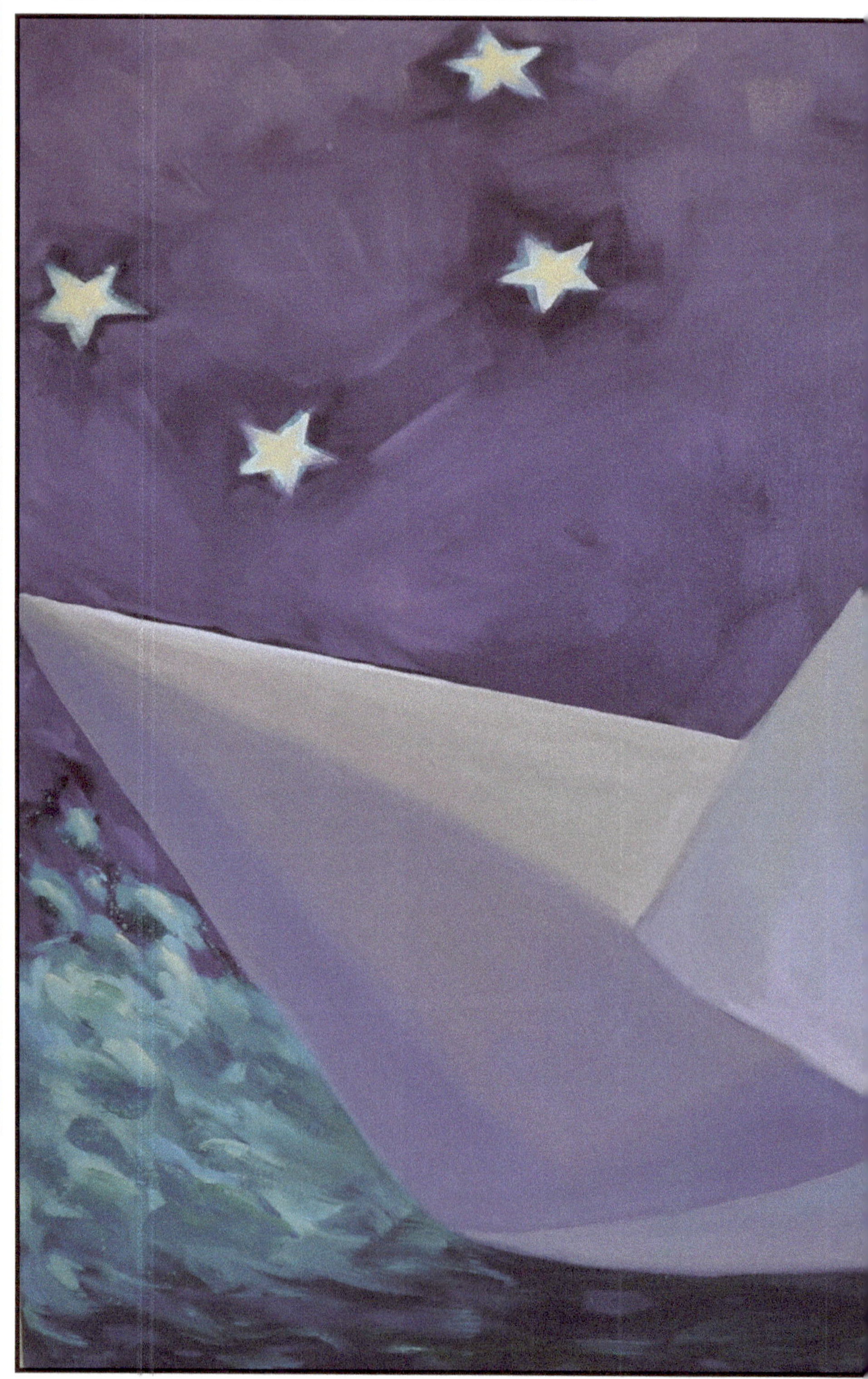

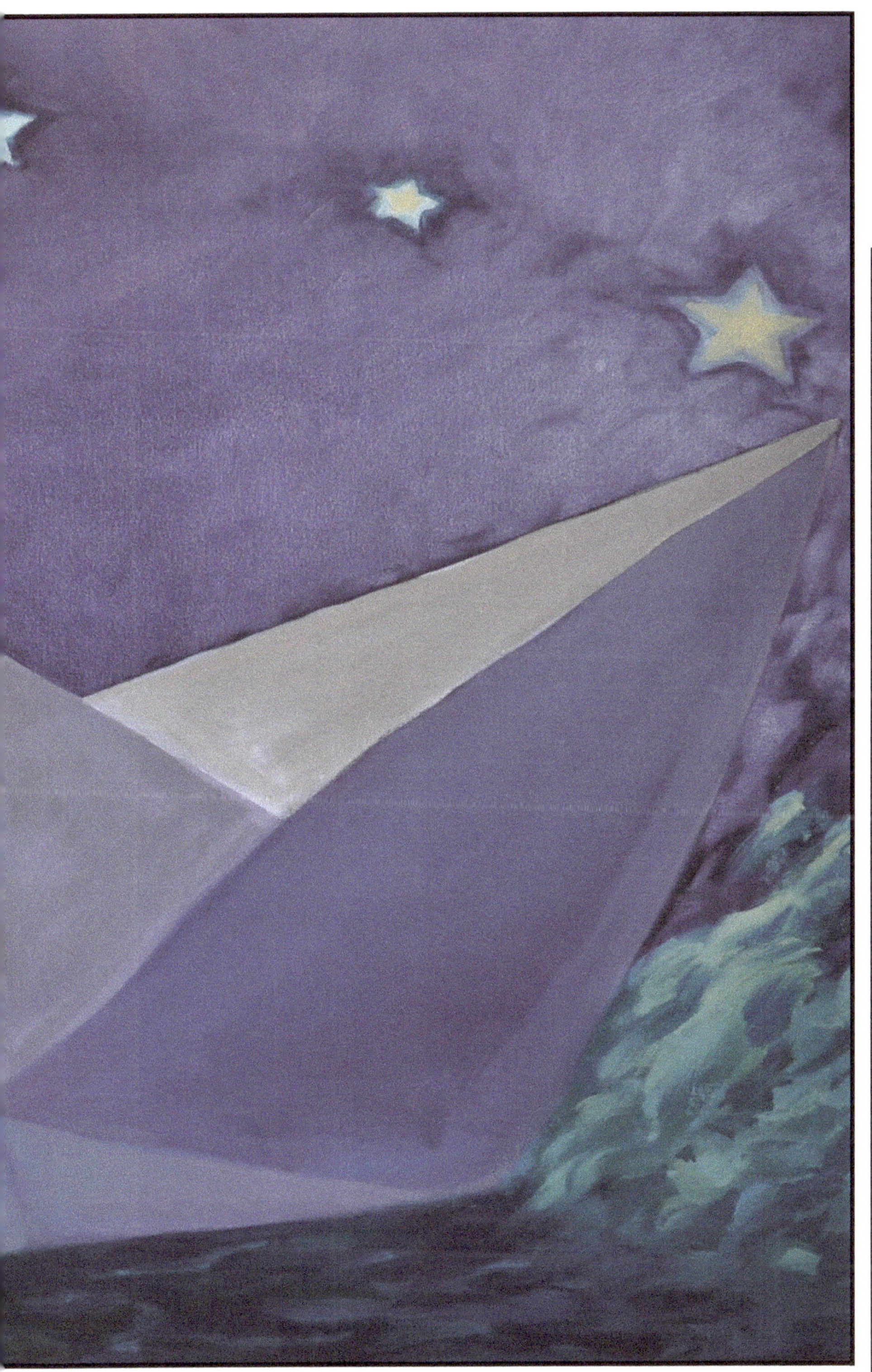

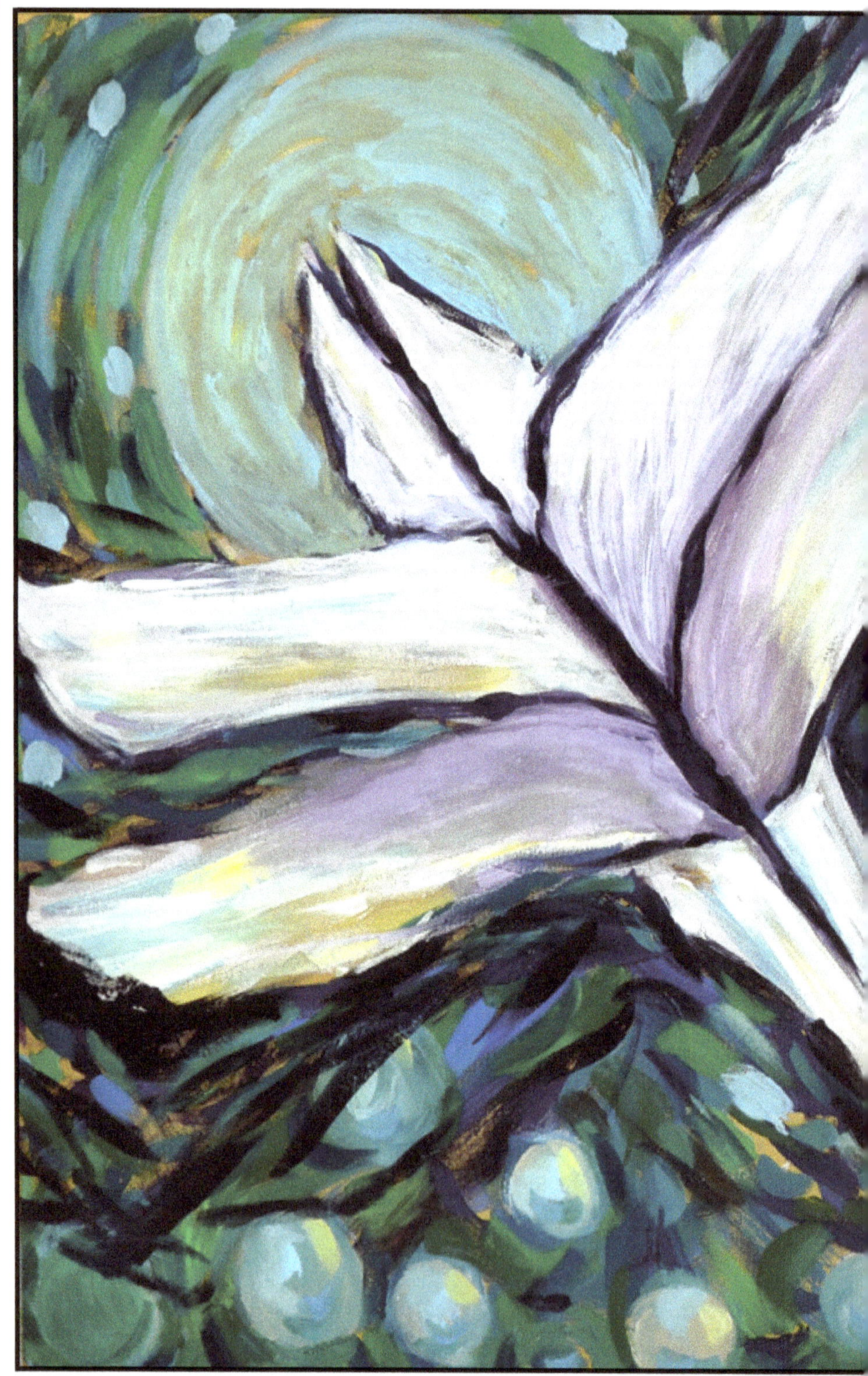

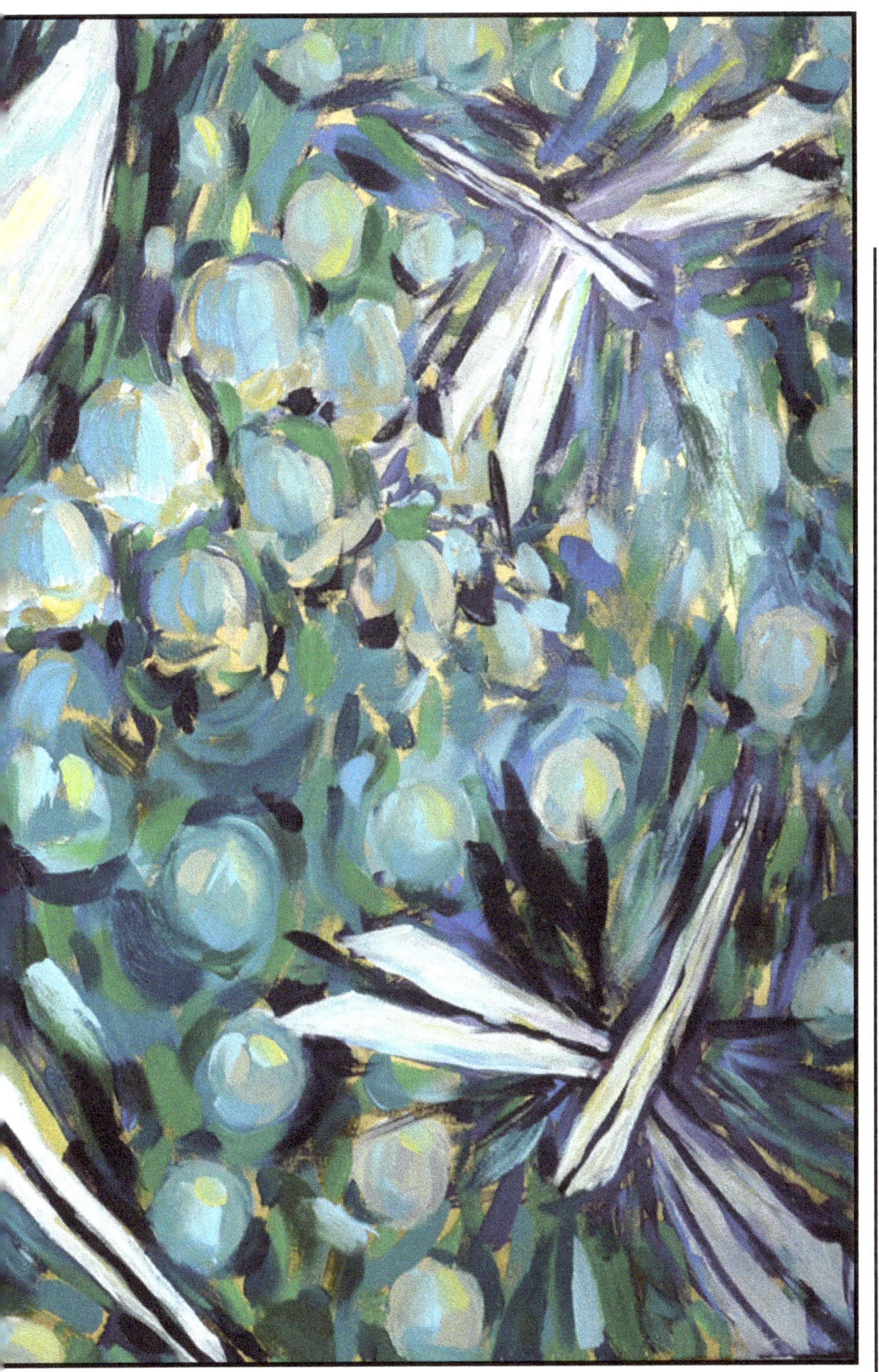

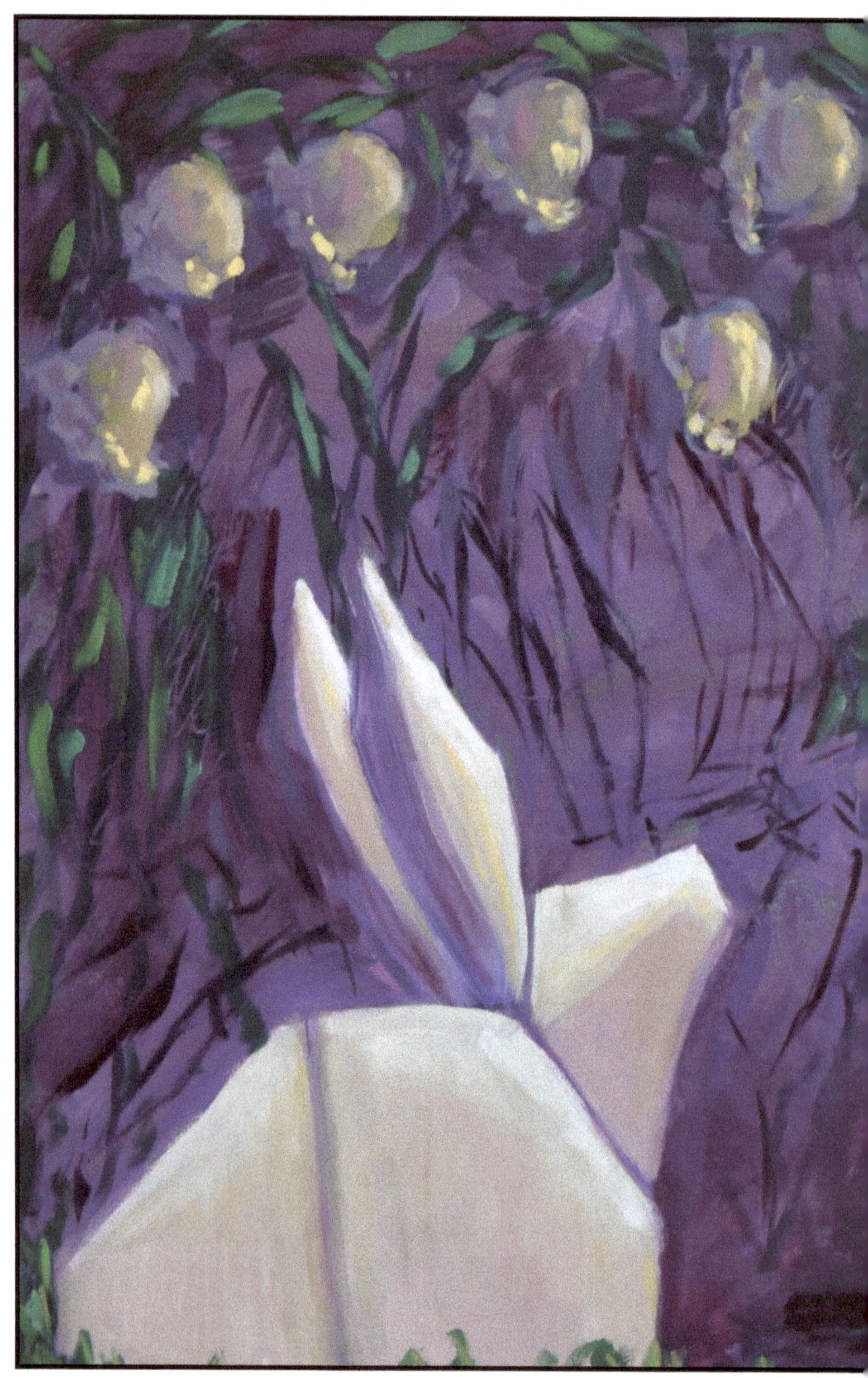

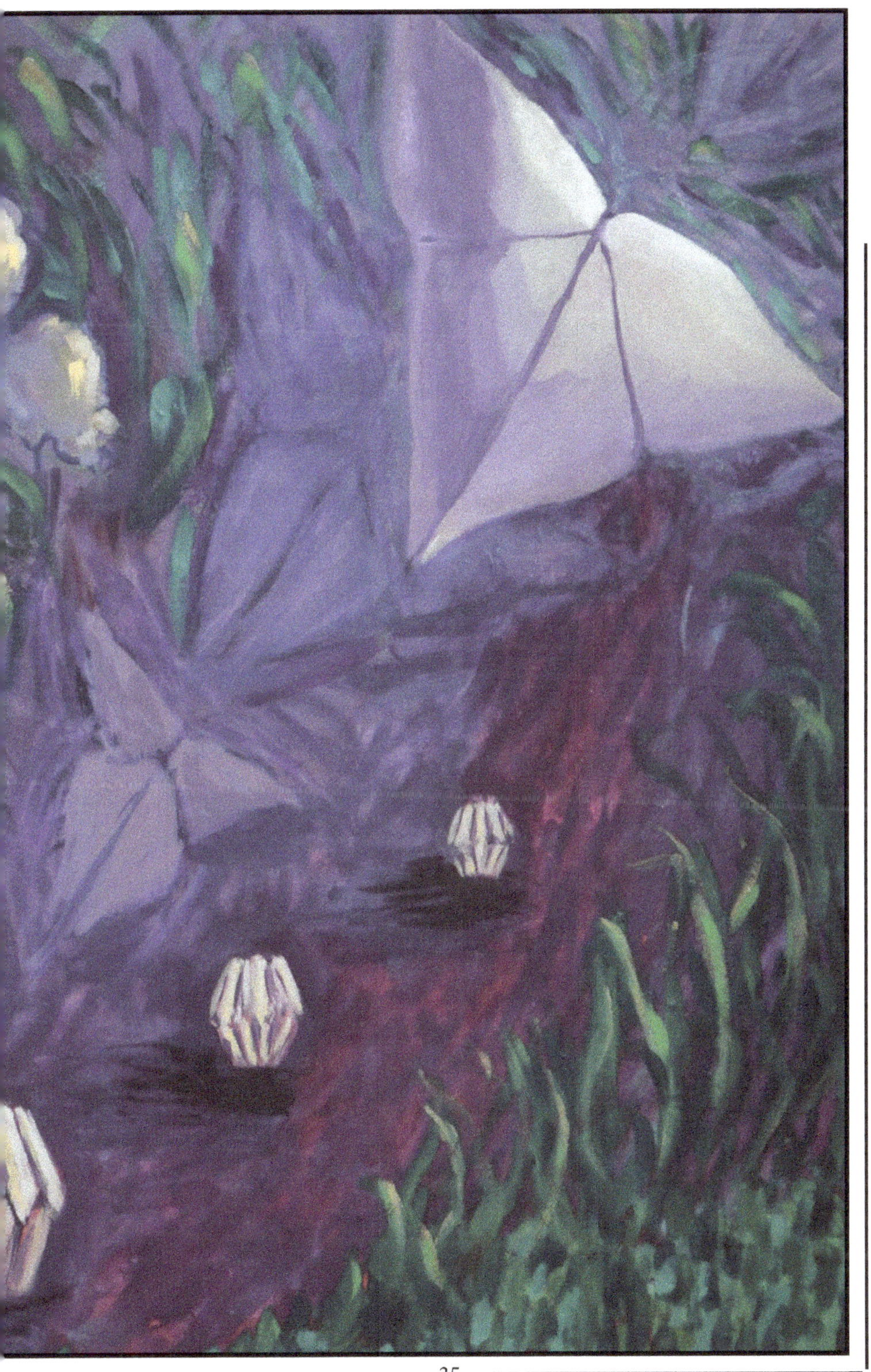

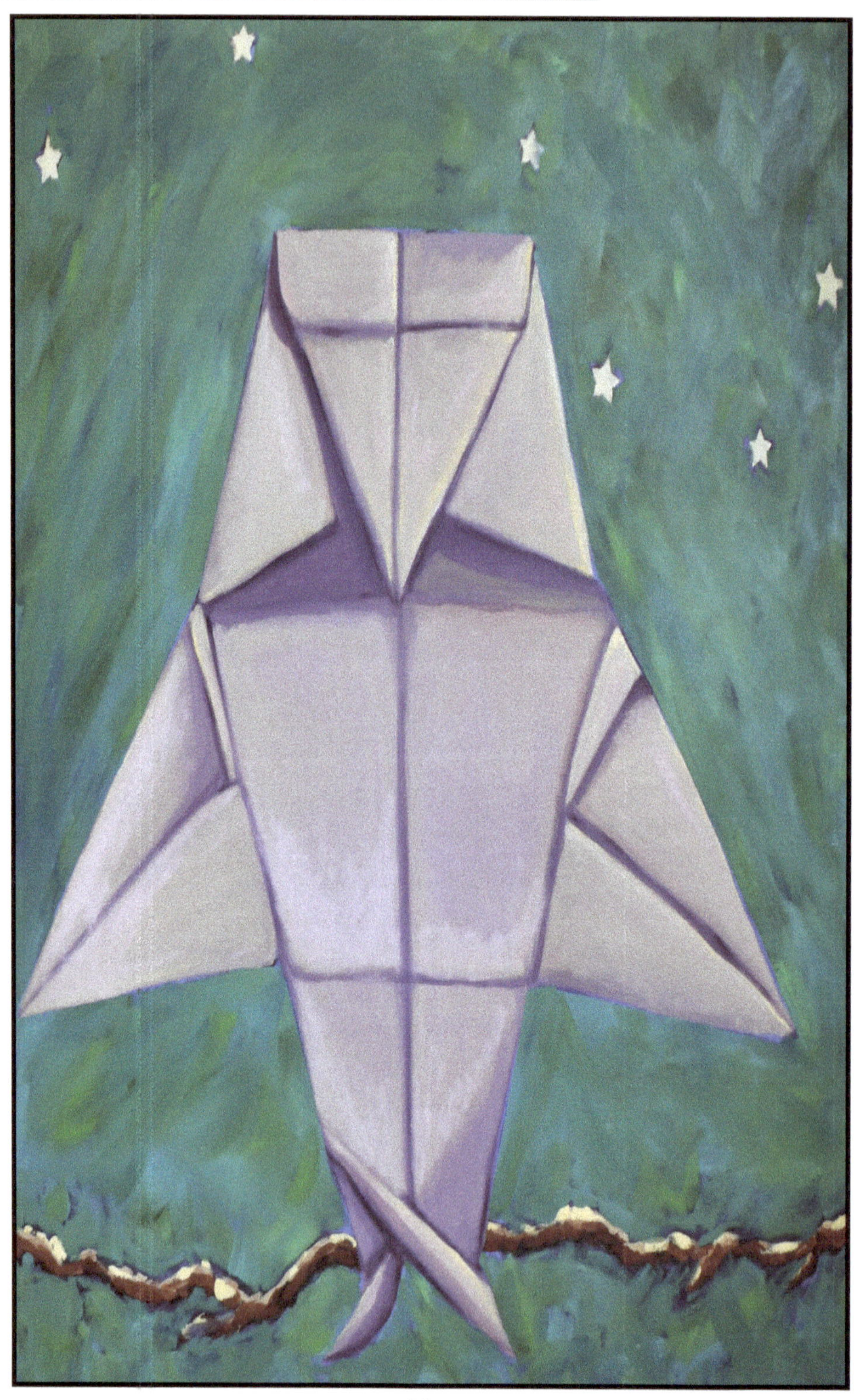

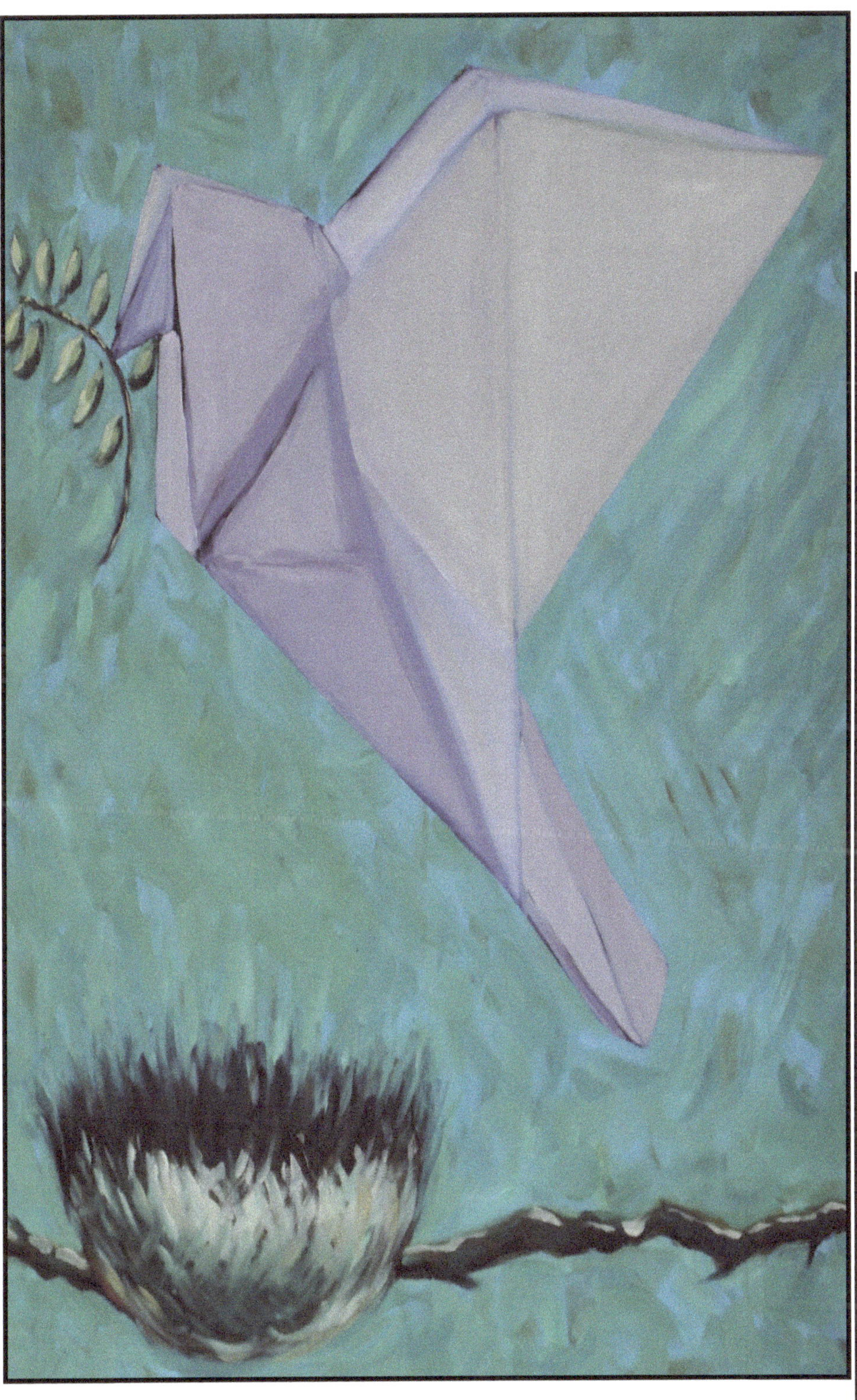

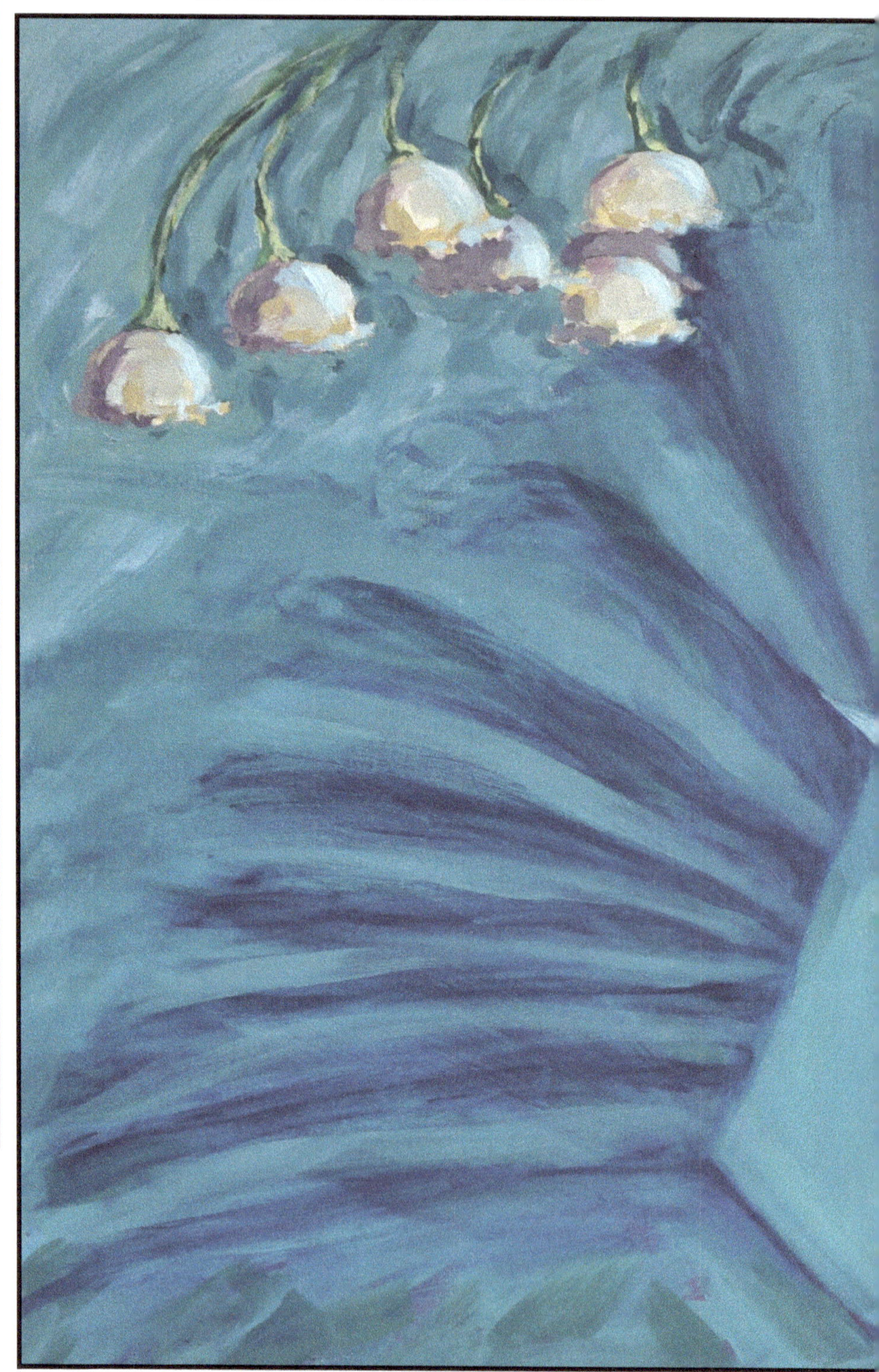

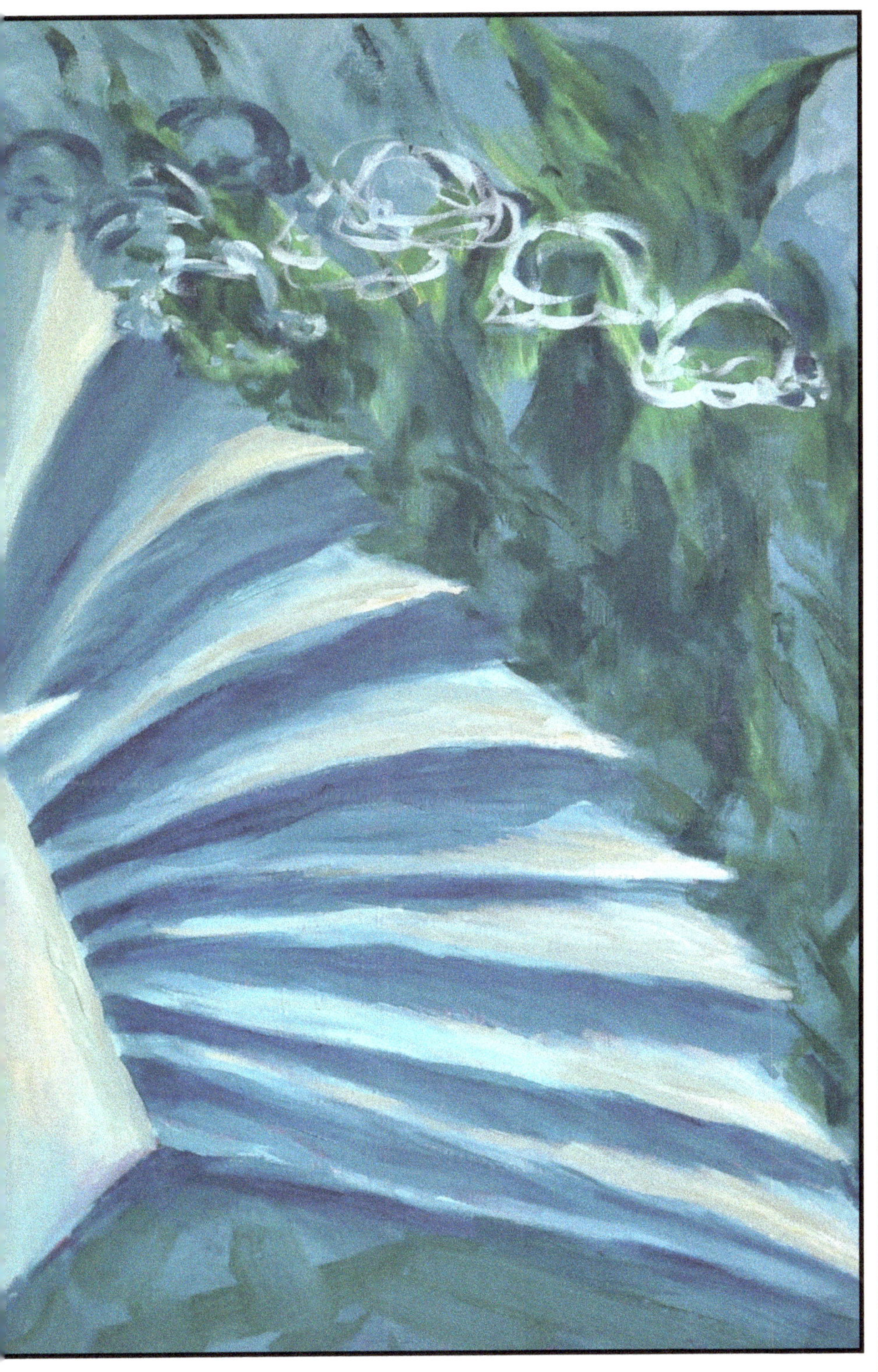

RABBIT CROSSING: 2020

Stuart Terman

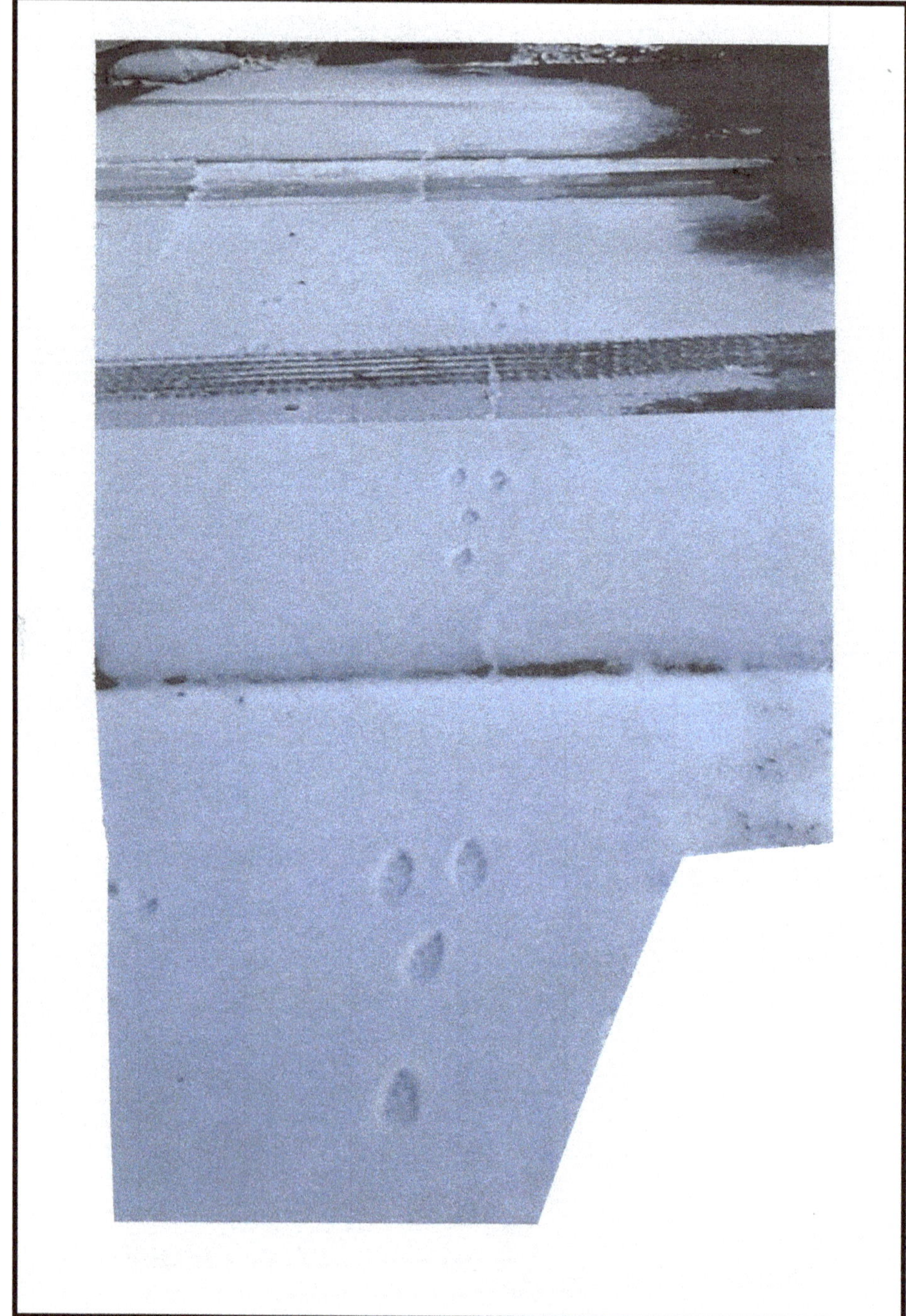

Walking Again

Erin Block

No one wanted the feet til May
When we all started walking again
on dry ground like we'd been at sea
And our legs, still wobbly,
Carried us out the door
to our first sunburn of the year
So we could lay in bed
and feel warm under a flower moon
With the windows full open
Like it's later in the year than it is.

I'd put them on the snowbank
Covering the strawberry bed
On a January night
When other rabbits were making tracks
Still with their lucky feet.
But these stopped so fast when I shot,
The jackrabbit rolled like a kid down a hill
Grass stained
Dirt under nails
And I walked up to it so slow and sure
and hungry for that feeling again
I scolded myself for being so proud.

Now here's a chipmunk gnawing the tendons
like jerky men make
when they don't know how to cook
And here's a chickadee pulling hair for her nest
That will hole up in a big ponderosa
With warmth of rabbit fur
from hundreds of miles away
And thousands of feet downhill
From something foreign and special
From high-plains sand and sun and twilight
where you never hear the owl coming.

Every spring my mother would cut our hair,
Sitting on a bucket by the hitching post
Letting split ends fall like leaves
Back when everything wasn't pine
And everything wasn't gray

And one day she cut until my head felt so light,
When I turned to look away from home
There wasn't anything tying me back there anymore.

My mother called my sister Chickadee
Because she never stayed in the same place long
Hey, sweetie
Hey, sweetie
Why are you running?
And I said to my sister, You lead the way.

The haircuts were all straight lines
Across our backs and foreheads
Like marks on the door jamb to measure height
Until maybe she decided
it was better not to know how far we'd grow apart.

She always put our hair out for the birds
Like her mother did hers
And her mother before that
And this was our tradition
A way we could talk
Without saying the ways we hurt.
Each strand of brown and gray, and gold
Threads of a story we didn't have to tell
Once it was part of something newer and younger
braided in with brome grass.

But we never thought of how nests fall from the sky
And usually right where they were made too.

Now my mother says Call your grandmother
She'll remember you.
But I know this is the one thing
That can't be true if it has to be spoken.
I know people forget people
And how to be one in the end.

Postman

Marj Hogan

My granddad delivered from Vanport to Rochester, on the Ohio
River. Rain, snow, sleet, hail / they said he was the first
Catholic postman in Beaver County / and by this I understood
that he made an opening in a once-closed thing, though from

a century on, the opening seems so obvious: inevitable, even.
Sleet, snow, hail, rain / an immigrant son puts on a uniform,
and becomes the country. How else could our letters have
landed? A man punches a clock, makes his route / goes home,

feeds children. Six days a week the mail arrives, same box,
same hand, same hour. Snow, sleet, rain, hail / I want to ask him,
which of these things is inevitable, the sorting, the feeding, the
hour, the threshold, and which of these / at every step took effort?

Python or Snakes

Anna Winham

this is the language
in which you build
a world you already know,
you insist
no imagination.
syntax simple
constraint/structure   like
sonnets/sestinas   like
strangulation   no   blood supply.

this is the language
in which i build,
write what i perhaps don't know.
i image like
slipping out of old skin.

where are your former selves?
the worlds you have built,
are they old worlds now,
obsolete operating systems,
memories, archives, correspondence
collections of figures
whose history we find too small   constricting
for our violent craving?
how do you build a world
always in motion? how do you
imagine a man still
inside his skin?

Alter Ego

Andrea Jones

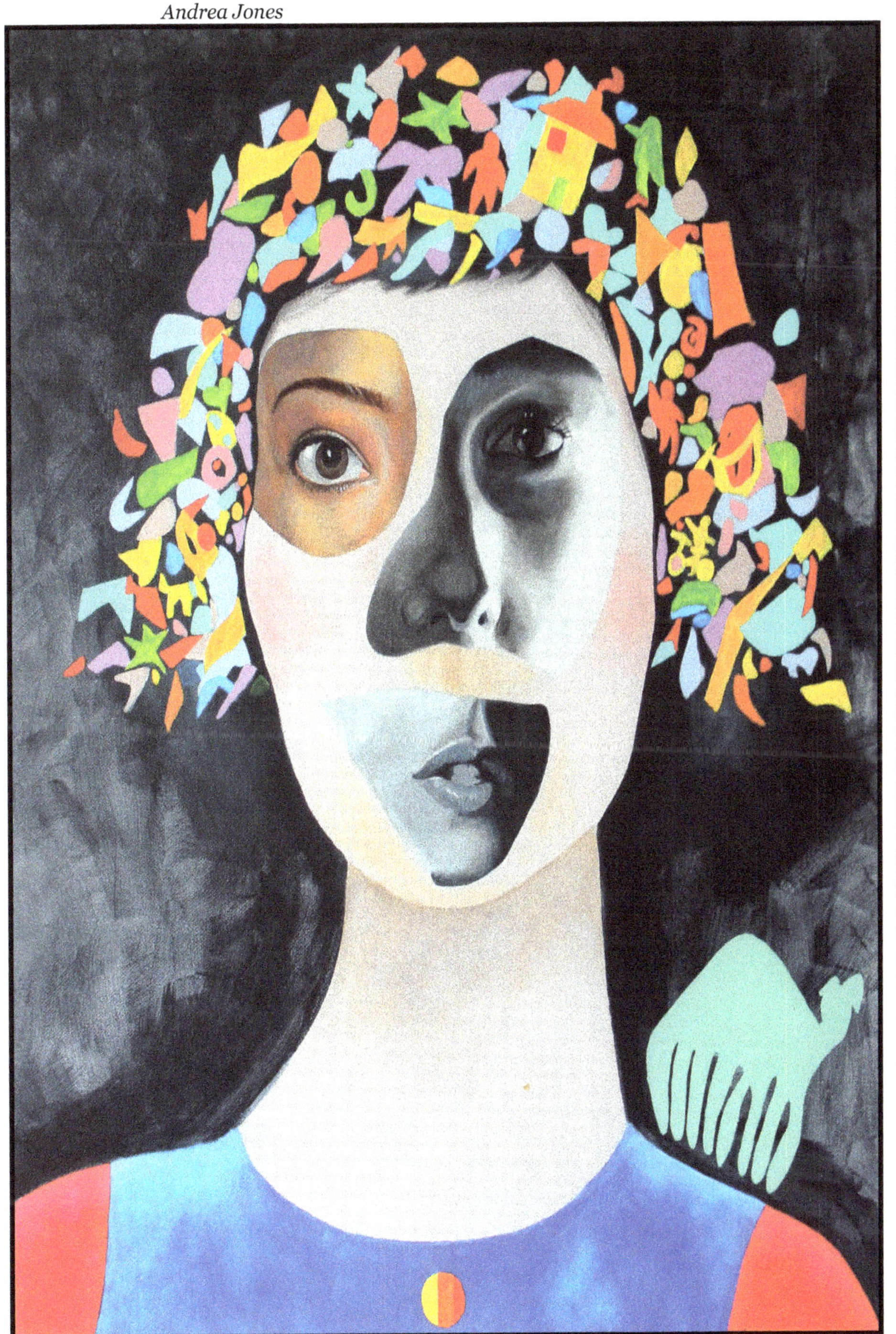

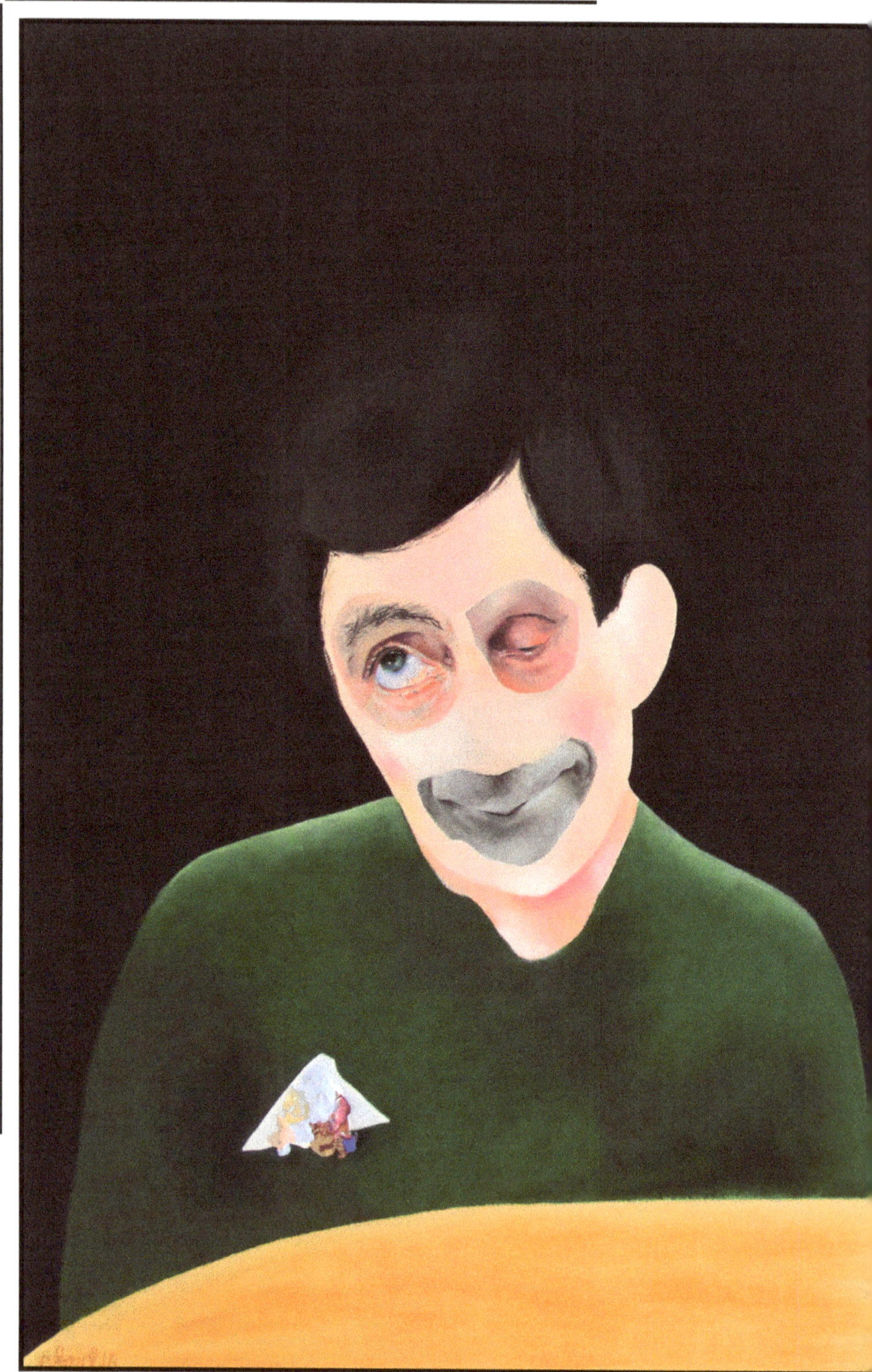

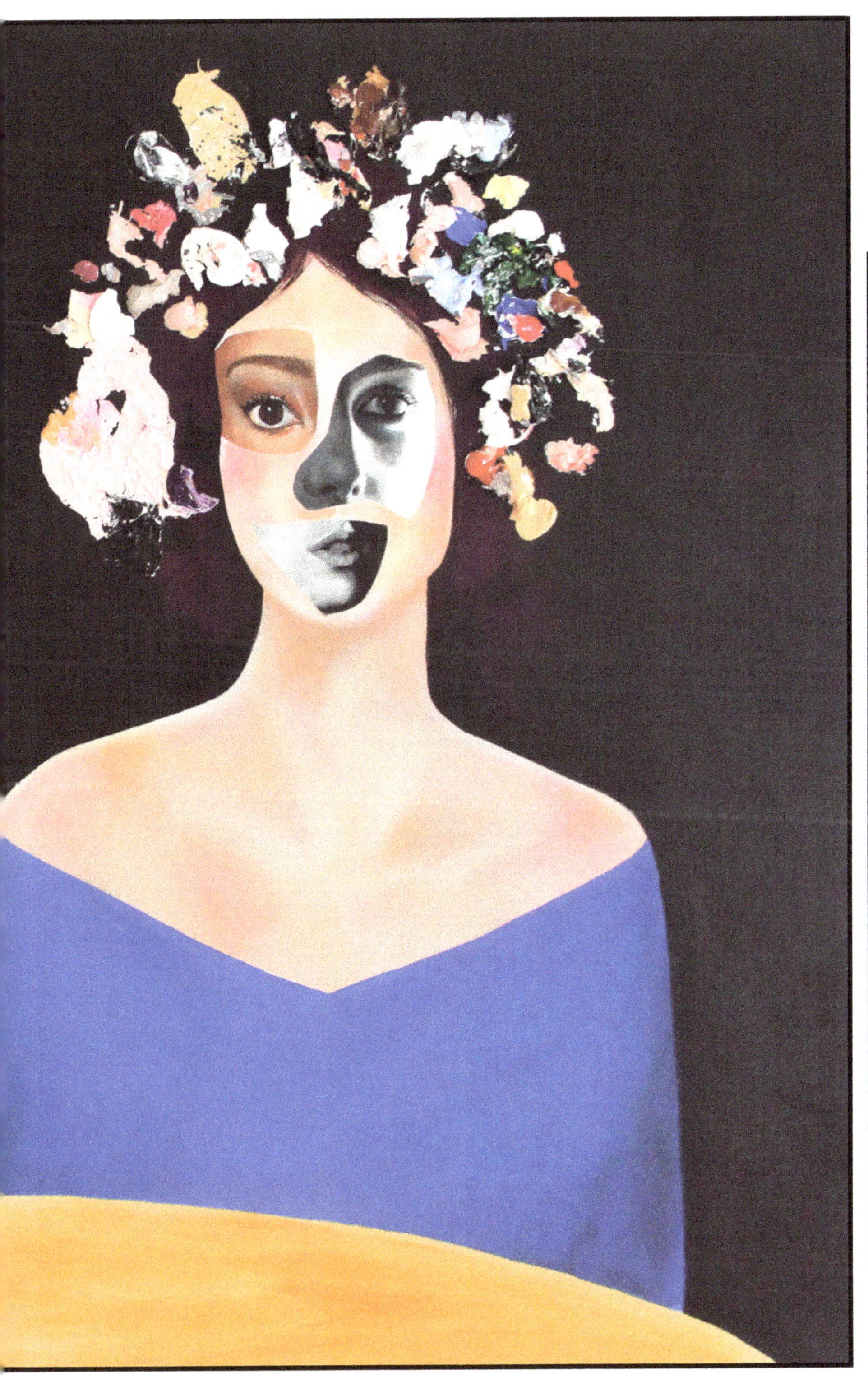

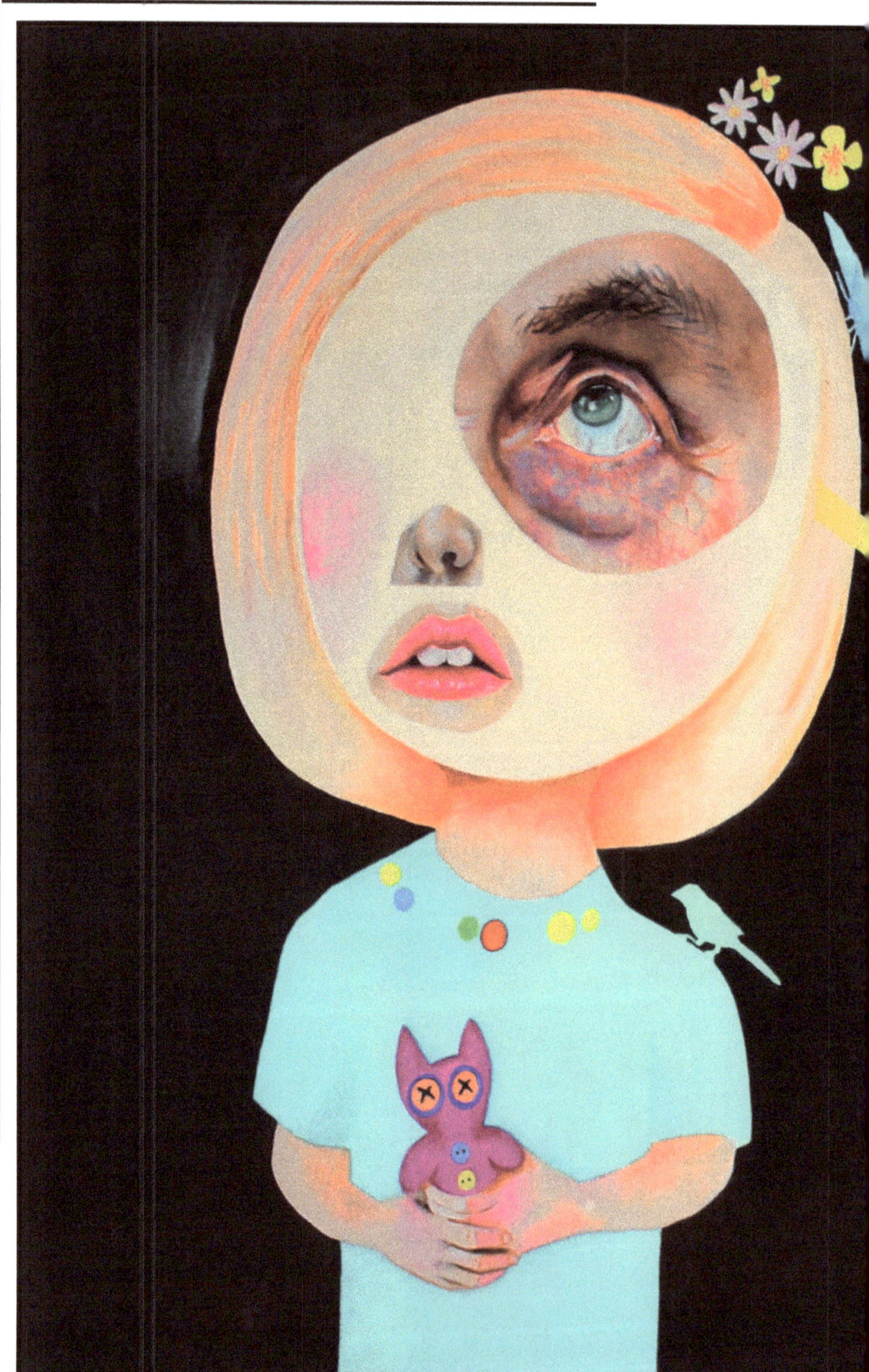

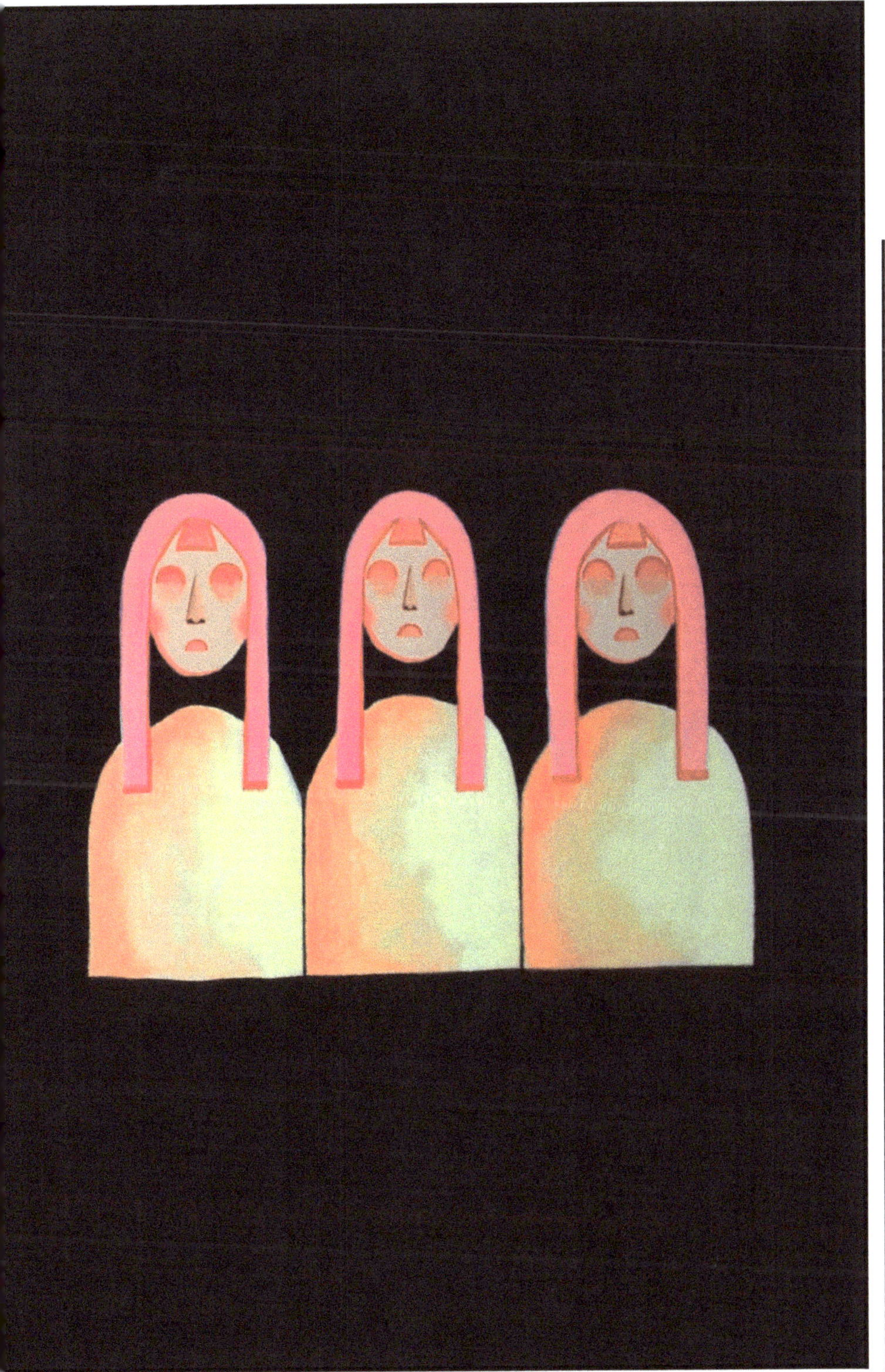

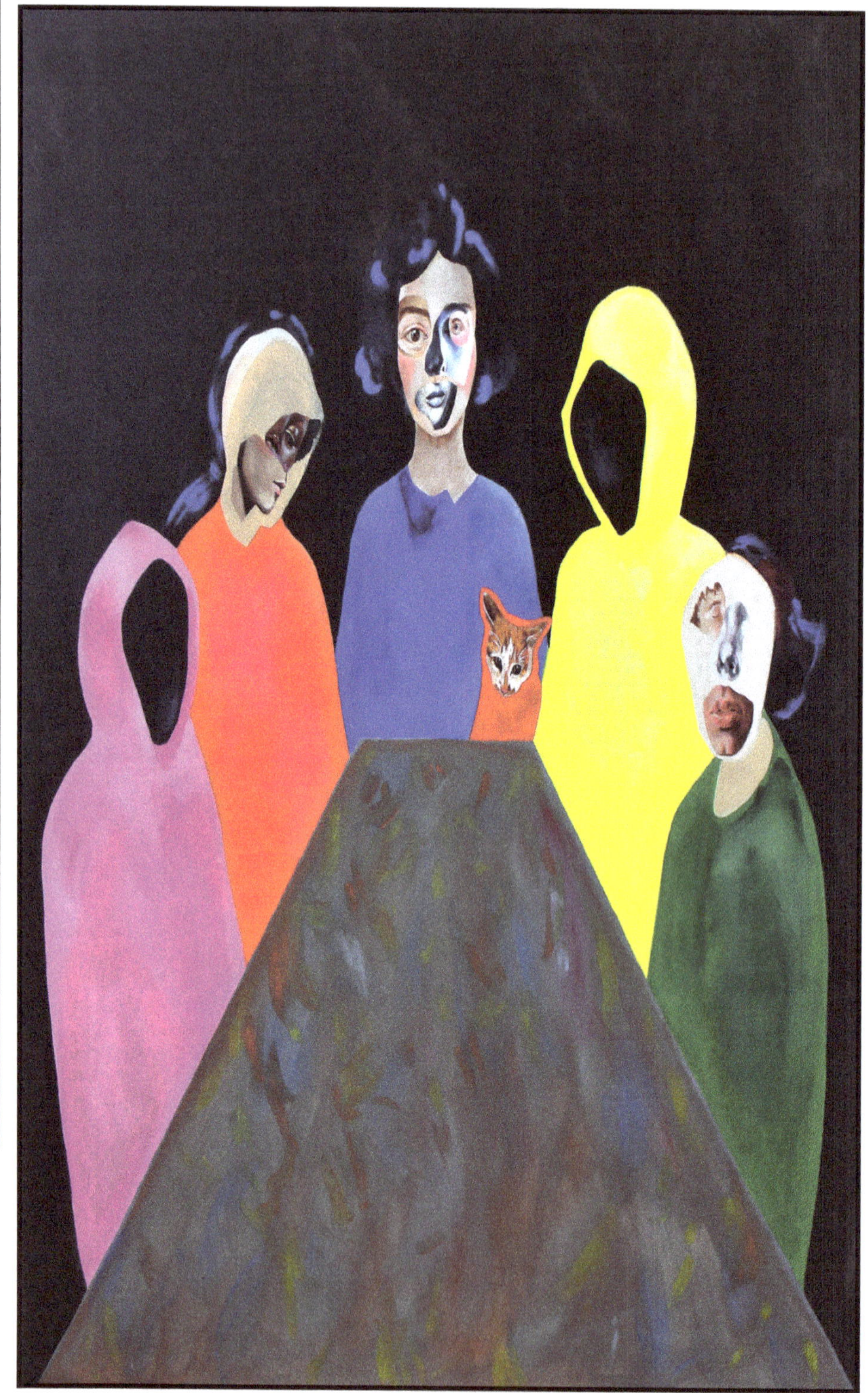

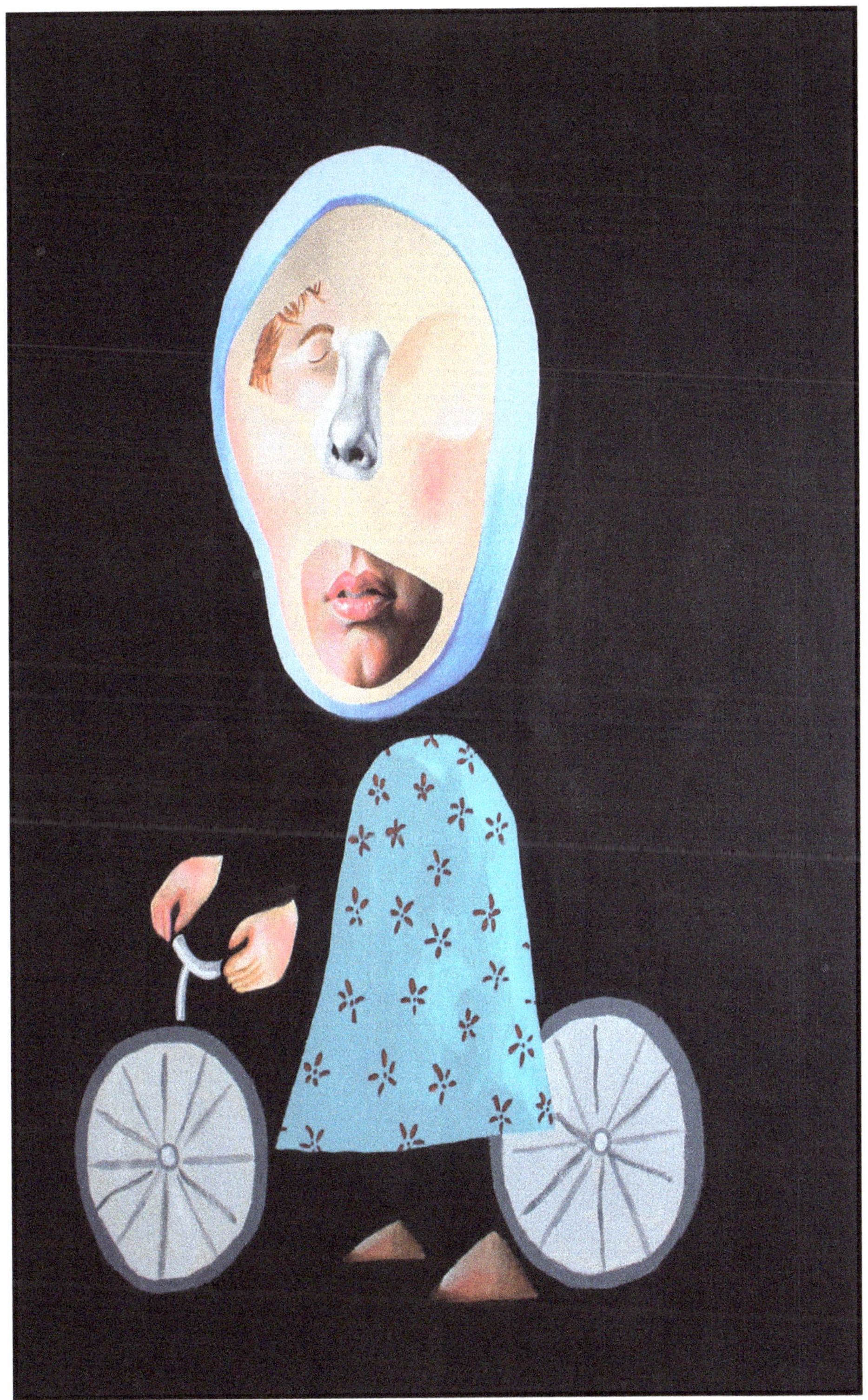

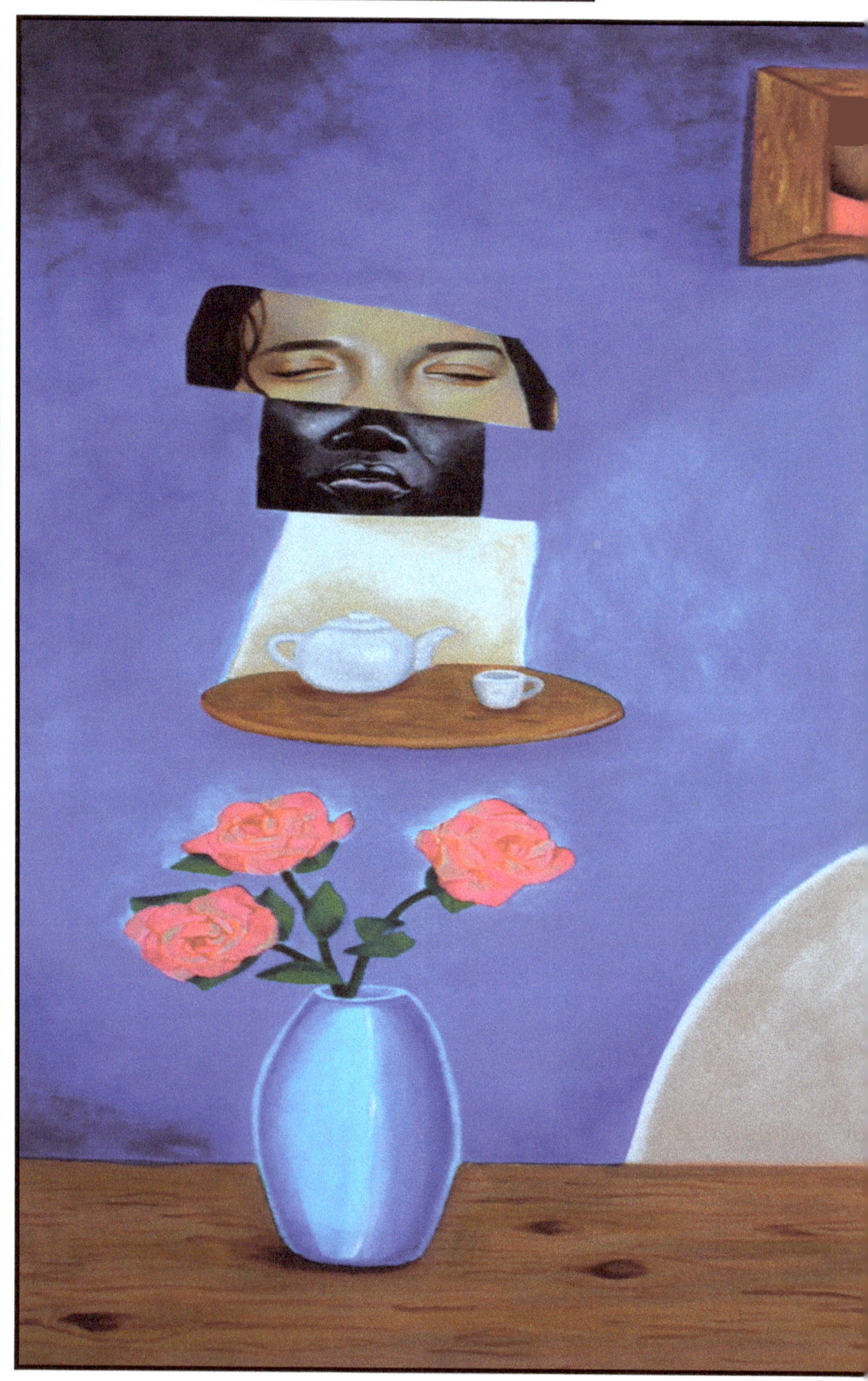

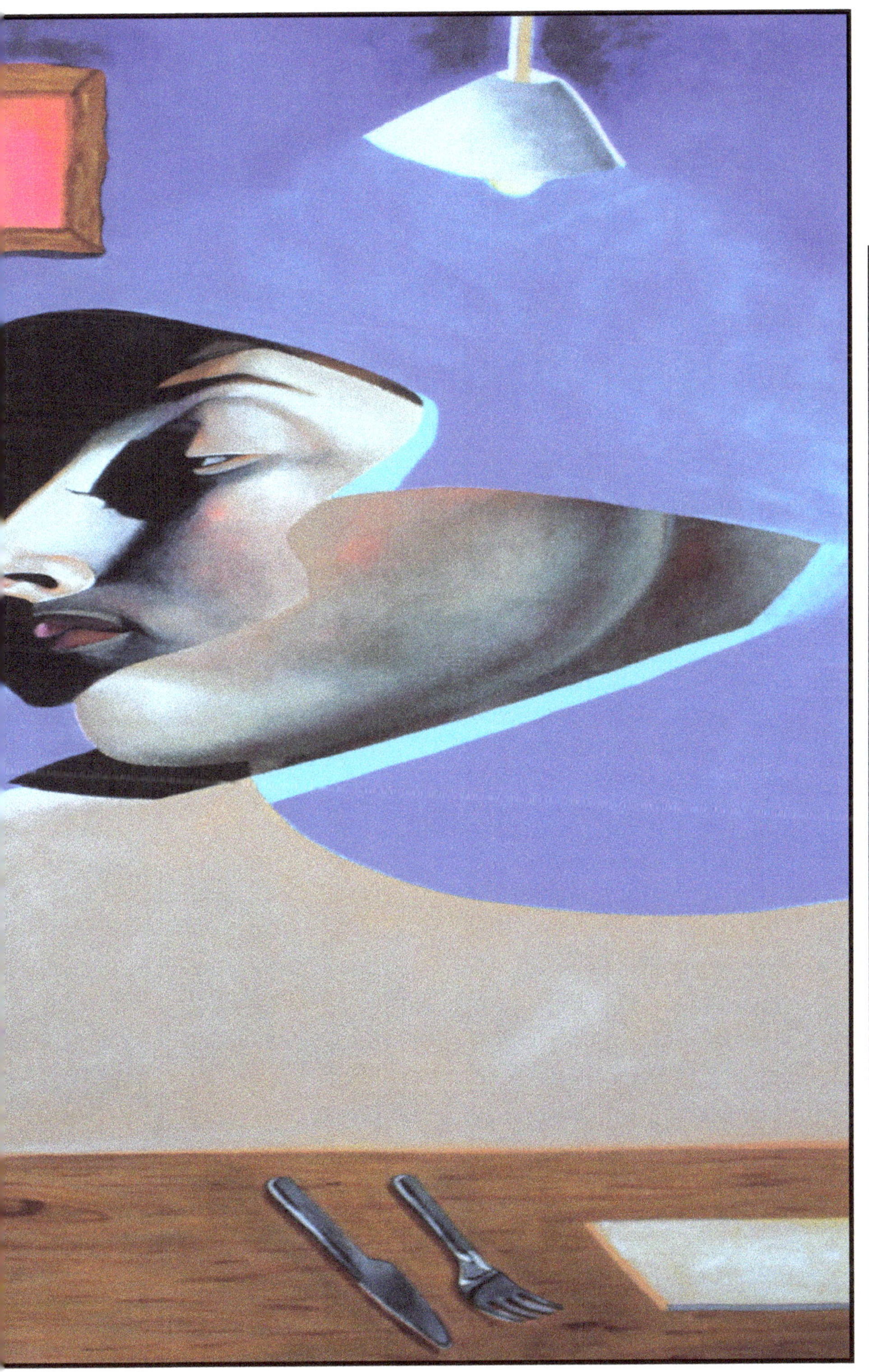

Thank You So Much for Inviting Me to Your Party

Ellie Lynch

Hi! Thanks so much for inviting me to your party. I didn't have anything to do tonight and was actually planning on journaling and/or emotionally spiraling by candlelight until about 3:25 AM. This is good for me. I needed to get out of the house.

Sooo, so sorry to interrupt your conversation but I literally don't care what you're talking about at all. You're the only person I know here though so I'm just going to talk really fervently about myself towards you if that's cool. Hope you don't mind if I tell you really intimate details about all the people I've ever been in love with before launching into a rant about how important it is to "invest in good skincare" like a condescending soccer mom. Just trying to help :)

Do you know where the bathroom is in this place? I don't need to go at all, but it seems like something I could do later. Maybe it could be the climax in this three-act dramedy that is Me Stepping Out of the House and Attending an Event with Real-Life People (it's getting developed into a mini-series starring Julianne Moore as me, and by that I mean I emailed HBO about the idea but they haven't gotten back to me yet. "Give it time," I whisper to myself every morning into my very black—yes, black!—coffee, "Give it time.")

What was that? Oh, you called this party "absolute chaos?" I agree. But you do know the etymology of the word *chaos*, don't you? Oh, you don't? Well, it's actually a term borrowed from Ancient Greek meaning "infinite darkness" or "void." (I pause for a second after; my brow is furrowed as if to say *I have more depth than you.* Then, I actually say that out loud accidentally. Oops!) I have more depth than you.

The ambience in this room reminds me of an underground speakeasy. I went to one with a friend once when I was travelling abroad in Europe. You can't even imagine what it was like walking down those stairs – what? You have to go? Don't you want to hear me tell the rest of this adorable anecdote? I have pictures! You probably won't understand them though because it takes a real photographer's eye to notice the contrast of light and dark—and you're gone.

Well, this was fun. And it's only midnight, which means that I definitely have time to take a bubble bath and think very hard about why all of my previous relationships have failed. (I'm a free spirit/too multi-dimensional to be understood/I refuse to put down my Moleskine, et cetera.)

Please let me know the next time you all are getting together. I'd love to catch up over matcha and by that I mean I'd love to hold you hostage in a coffee shop while reciting confessional poetry at you that I wrote during my Intro to Philosophy class. You'll love it! See you later! And don't forget all the stuff I told you about that expensive face serum with the fish eggs. It's super exfoliating.

Official Statement from Women Advocating for Microwave Meals (WAMM)

Claire Franken

Sitting at home on a Thursday evening, after days of lying on the couch re-watching old seasons of *Project Runway* you've already seen, eating dinner becomes a chore. Even after weeks of staying at home, you may feel an obligation to maintain just the slightest degree of normalcy by eating three meals a day at normal times. I, too, feel this sense of obligation at times. I ignore it every time.

I cannot cook. The last real meal I concocted was a tuna noodle casserole, the most basic of all casseroles. It has like three ingredients. The experience still managed to be a harrowing one, as I burned my hand four times and the finished product tasted like flavorless baby food. I was less than pleased. "Tuna Noodle Gate," as I like to call it, explains why I am a strong advocate for microwave dinners.

Implementing the microwave dinner diet is easier than you think. You may be wondering, ok, that's fine for lunch and maybe dinner, but what about breakfast? Don't worry! They make several microwave breakfast sandwiches, burritos, and scrambles, so your diet will include non-dinner foods as well! Replacing every meal with a frozen dinner is life changing, and for those who need a little extra push, I've comprised a list of advice to ease this lifestyle transition during these weeks at home.

1. Meal prepping a microwave dinner is absolutely crucial. You must mentally prepare yourself to spend only 10 minutes at most for both preparing and eating the meal. This may seem difficult since right now you may be dedicating anywhere between 45 minutes to an hour of your day to cooking and eating. The best way to eliminate these extra minutes is to busy yourself with studying, class, or work;

you cannot tempt yourself with extra time. It's best to operate in a perpetual state of frantic rush.

2.   Become fond of crusty, burnt cheese. You can practice eating this in the weeks leading up to your transition. Any frozen dinner that incorporates cheese, which is common, overcooks on the sides and creates a hard ring around your cuisine. So, simply overcook grilled cheese or pizza on the stove before implementing the microwave dinner diet so you can slowly introduce your body to this new flavor experience.

3.   Do not go grocery shopping, ever. Only shop at convenience stores like CVS or Rite Aid. These kind of establishments will not tease you with "organic fruit," or "freshly baked goods." Do not even waste your time with grabbing a basket. Microwave meals are packaged in user friendly boxes that can easily be stacked and stuffed into your arms. Again, remain in a state of panic and rush even while purchasing the meals.

4.   Do not be vegetarian or vegan while implementing the microwave diet. You will feel like you're merely eating a small snack if you don't indulge in those hearty dinners filled with unidentifiable chunks of protein.

5.   Do not be Italian or Hispanic while implementing the microwave diet. The pastas and enchiladas will not meet your standards.

6.   Buy a new microwave so you know the exact wattage. You don't want to be stressed over deciding which directions to follow. Although the difference in cooking time between a 1000 Watt and 800 Watt

microwave seems minimal, every second counts when preparing your Lean Cuisine. That being said, if you don't know the wattage, just throw out the directions and set the timer to "popcorn" and take out the meal when it begins to smoke.

7. Satisfy your cravings. If you're having a tough day and think you may need the comfort of a freshly baked cookie, don't give up on the diet! Betty Crocker does make microwavable brownie and cake treats. I recommend eating these in secret, though, because chocolate will stick to all of your teeth. This may unsettle your friends who then may encourage you to switch back to a regular, human diet which will most certainly affect your progress.

8. Just get rid of your oven! Throw it away, don't even donate it or sell it. You don't want to encourage other Americans to cook. In an age where phones and laptops keep getting smaller and smaller and more packed with power, ovens should be the next good to modernize. A microwave is small, can be unplugged, moved to any room (do not hesitate to clear a space on your bedside table in the event that you need a midnight snack in bed) and is so powerful it can cook an entire frozen turkey dinner! It's really the only appliance womankind needs.

I myself only eat meals that I know have undergone cryogenic freezing by liquid nitrogen, been vacuum packed into one single tray, and been processed with the proper seasoning of extra salt and fat. If every American dedicated themselves to following this diet, rates of being hangry would drastically decrease and there would be less kitchen related injuries. So, take the plunge! Unplug that dirty, dust collecting dinosaur of an appliance formally known as an "oven."*

*Results may vary.

Abstinence, Only...?

Laurie Rosenwald

You thought it went away? Well, think again.

Trump's budget proposed eliminating the Teen Pregnancy Prevention Program, and he's appointed Valerie Huber, former president of the National Abstinence Education Association, to the Department of Health and Human Services, which is like the NHS except it rates 27th in the world, and asthma, heart failure, hypertension, and diabetes are increasing exponentially. Future TPPP recipients will be expected to implement abstinence-only priorities.

Ms. Huber, a well-known nincompoop, is known to support programs like WAIT, an acronym for "Why Am I Tempted," whose training videos included this priceless sound byte:

"Girls' brains are like spaghetti, boys' brains are like waffles... girls cradle schoolbooks like a baby...boys pursue girls and girls wait to be pursued by boys...we have a generation of girls looking for daddy love...you just have to get that sperm close to her vagina and she turns on the little Hoover vacuum, because girls are very, very fertile..." See?

In light of this boneheaded "Abstinence-Only" policy in schools, and as a former teenager—and apparent slut—I thought it was the very least I could do to present a fairly informative, kind of accurate, but not nearly comprehensive account of, well... you know. If kids learn just a few of the ghastly, disgusting "facts," they'll be less likely to try to find out all of them, through the internet and stuff. Or even worse, experience. A little misinformation goes a long way. In an effort to increase the sensual pleasure of anxious, frustrated parents and guide, educate and inform their clueless, frustrated, and nubile offspring, I offer the following report:

Where Babies Really Come From

The sexual act is best demonstrated by putting your finger into an electrical outlet. First you must wet your finger. See? Sex is very painful and may cause an "organism." An organism might pop out and make you scream something like, "Lupe Fiasco," "Espèce de coloquinte à la graisse d'anthracite!" or "Deutsche Grammophon Gesellschaft!" Then the organism turns into a tadpole. If you are wearing rubber, don't worry, because you are grounded, and protected from the organism.

Before the sexual act, put on new sneakers and brush your tongue. Start up your Tom Jones record and try some French Twisting. Depending on your

Operating System, you may experience one or more side effects, such as diaper rash, global thermonuclear meltdown, or tummy ache.

Try not to drool on your sex partner. This may cause a short. To practice safe sex, I recommend Malware Bytes 3.6, and a Panamax-9-Outlet Surge Protector. Now, close your eyes, open your mouth, and get ready for the ride of your life. All right then... Awaaay we go!

Some believe sex is where babies come from, but we now know that babies come from France. Sex is like something you feel for a pet, only not nearly as intense and erotic. It is much like love, but if done correctly, burns even more calories. True love can last up to fourteen minutes, but good sex can last for years at a time.

Avoid sex with dead people. This is called Philadelphia, and is frowned upon. If you have sex with your relatives, you'll have to light incense. Instead, have sex over the phone or through your computer. It's clean, efficient and modern. For some reason our telecommunication devices seem unwilling to perform even the most basic sexual services, but we just noticed the laser printer winking at us. It seems to be warming up, so we're taking it to Alain Ducasse at The Dorchester on Friday for a microfiber rubdown, nozzle cleaning and a late supper in the Salon Prive.

People enjoy sex in many different ways. Some people are into pain. Others are into peanut. This is called M&M's, and either way, cutie, it's going to hurt like Hell.

You can make big money with sex, but only in Las Vegas. Nevada is the only state where the constitution is legal. If someone offers you a "job" for twenty dollars, talk them down to ten. For oral sex you'll need a muffler, Peppersmith Spearmint Chewing Gum, and some felt. You can even have sex with yourself if you have a subscription to "SCOOTERING" Magazine. This is called procrastination, and the Catholics believe it is very naughty. Feel free to have sex with up to twelve people, but only if they are condescending adults. Sex is like ballroom dancing, except Claudia Winkleman is not always complaining about your short neck, and you don't have to wear your hair in a bun. Also, I happen to know from experience that Russians are no better at it than regular people.

For more information, BBC Springwatch is good, except for the spiders, unless you really hate your boyfriend. Kangaroos have three vaginas, but this is not particularly relevant, or even remotely helpful, for teenagers or anybody else. I feel differently about them now. I don't even know why I mentioned it. I am sorry.

With sex, remember that size is the most important thing. If you are the size of a muon or a quark, forget it. Nobody's going to be sexually attracted to a sub-atomic particle they can't even see.

Nota Bene: if you have sex with a minority, you might even go to jail, because they are much too young. There you will have brutal sex with a man with a tattoo on his bicep that says "mother." You will meet him in the shower if you drop the soap, and then you will be his "girl" even if you are a boy. This is what they call being "inmate" with somebody. It is said that the ancient Greeks started this trend, which, after 3000 years, is still as popular as ever!

If you wear lots of clothing, no one will have sex with you. If you wear tiny tri-angles of cloth attached with string, they will be all over you. If you are a boy, any young girl with two big houseplants will "turn you on." You will become hard like a rock all over and if you don't have sex right away somebody's going to have to mop up the kitchen. Probably you.

Everybody involved is to have at least one organism. But you can have as many as you want. The more organisms, the better!

If sex is so much fun, we asked, um, a "friend" why she doesn't "do it" more often. She said she couldn't find the "right guy." Apparently, he has to be "sin-gle." And "straight." We pointed out that New York City, where she lives, has the highest density of "singles" on earth, except for Kala-u-papa, that leper colony in Hawaii.

She told us to shut up, and that Sartre was right. She's been very moody. Perhaps she is molting. We tried to help, but she said she wouldn't have sex with us even if we weren't the size and shape of a Zamboni machine. Too bad, because she's one hot, sexy babe, and we could make her smooth and shiny all over.

Her parents were bohemian communists and told her about sex when she was six, but then she forgot, eventually learning it from Alan a few years later in Central Park, a few feet away from the statue of Daniel Webster, who support-ed the Compromise of 1850 which included the Fugitive Slave Law that re-quired federal officials to recapture runaway slaves. Why does this top asshole get a statue? Never mind.

If you look down, there's a small bronze plaque that marks the place where they did "it." That night she lost her flower, because it was the "sixties," when "flower power" was "happening." Unfortunately, she also lost her house keys, which is how her mother found out. Boy, was she mad! All mothers are against sex, but if they had not had sex they couldn't even be mothers. Unless, of course, they have been to France.

*This study could never have been completed without the expert advice of Mr. Graham Kerr, the "Galloping Gourmet," who, though not a registered sex therapist, has personally experienced sex, not once, but several times. I would also like to thank the world famous pianists, podiatrists, pediatricians, arachnids, marsupials and Brazilians who agreed to be interviewed for this article. Ignorant sluts Kate Upton, Emilia Clarke, Rosie Huntington-Whiteley, Deepika Padukone, Rihanna, Zendaya, Maya Jama, and The California Raisins all declined to be interviewed, as did Cybergirl of the Year Leanna Decker, and I would like to take this opportunity to publicly condemn and berate them.

want a beer?

Sean Gallagher

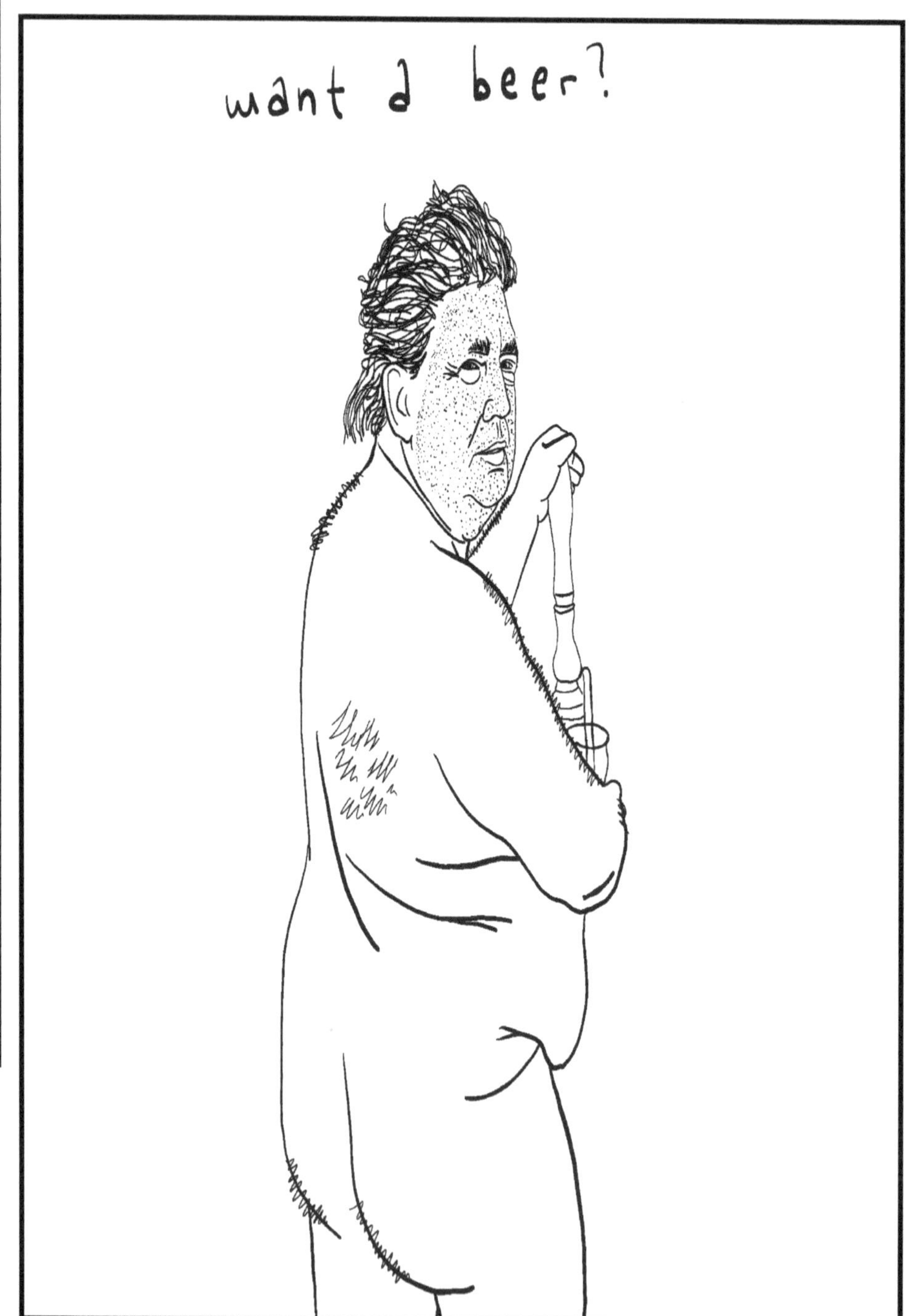

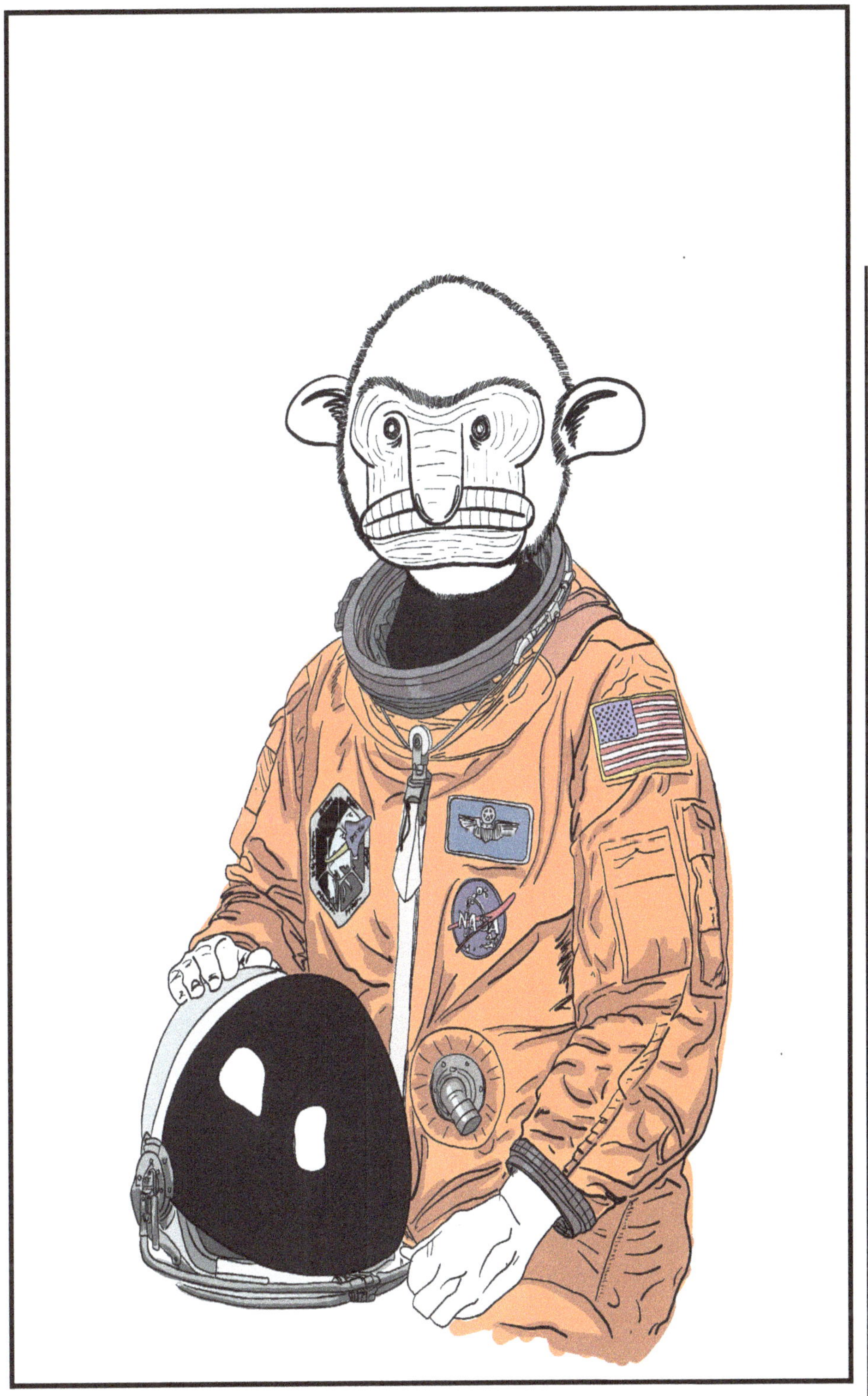

NASA

Plagapolis

Angus McLinn

Penalty Flag—Face Masking - Monday, March 16th, 2020

I pulled my facemask down and let it hang around my neck on a packed R train as it scraped its way out of Canal Street station. It was a little after nine in the morning and I'd already touched my face upwards of 30 times. After the Chinatown set disembarked, it became even more obvious that I was the only white guy with an N95 on and it was starting to make me uncomfortable. I figured the ones who weren't judging me for being paranoid were judging me for wasting medical equipment.

The train careened its way through the veins of Manhattan, punctuating the silence of the shoulder-to-shoulder commuter crowd with the irregular keening of air brakes and old-metal friction. At each station I refreshed newsfeeds that were already infected. Mass graves in Lombardy. Death trucks rolling through the barren streets of Chinese megacities, flanked by housing blocks sealed off by order of The State. A notification interrupted the end-times litany to inform me the morning meeting had been moved to conference room 301C as the crush of the crowd disgorged me onto the 42nd street platform.

It was the first meeting where we talked about death, and we became amateur numerologists. Friday the 13th had gone off without a hitch, but on Saturday an infamous, nameless woman with emphysema had died under a plastic sheet with a tube down her throat in a hospital somewhere in Brooklyn. She was 82-years young. The Ides of March had come a day early. The implications of all of this were not yet clear, but theories abounded. The only consensus was that it was a bad omen, although as far as pre-existing conditions went none of ours were that serious.

On my way home I stopped at Jimmy's bodega to pick up some beers and a pack of smokes. The old guys sipping Bud tall cans and counting each other's gin blossoms at the counter were familiar with numerology as well. They paid the state for some lucky numbers twice a day, and as far as I could tell they still weren't on the streets, so I figured that they had to know something.

Jimmy went to the fridge in back where he kept the cigarettes—"So they stay fresh," is what he told me once—wearing a pair of blue surgical gloves. I was waiting by the register watching my beers sweat when one old guy turned to another and said, "It's a death sentence from god." The second guy nodded, then let out a fearsome, dry cough.

Chat Noir - Monday, March 30th, 2020

I was trying to figure out if you're supposed to send a thank you note when you get a sympathy card or if you were exempt because you're trying not to dwell on your dead friends when my cat's smoker's cough kicked in. It seemed like every time I turned around she was hanging out the window, cackling at the squirrels on the fire escape in between drags. The cat thought the coronavirus was hilarious, even though she had already caught it like five times. When I told her she's gotta start taking this thing seriously she cackled that she had got four lives left and lit up another smoke.

It was a tightrope trying to keep her the hell off the streets and the internet at the same time. The day before I'd walked in on her in the middle of trying to start a Facebook group to protest social distancing. She wasn't always like this. I'd last lost her about a week ago, and I still wasn't sure if she was seriously trying to foment some sort of anti-public health rebellion or she was, "Just trolling," not that it mattered. She'd been drinking way too much, which made it harder to figure out if she was actually sick or just hung over. The whole thing was enough to make me start thinking that maybe I was the crazy one.

That afternoon I was on a conference call counting the recycling bags full of cans in my kitchen when I got tired of the dire arithmetic and left. The TV was on in the living room. I reflexively swiped at the mute button. It didn't matter. The TV was always on. I was always on mute. The cans had always been there. The only difference was now I had to live with them. I couldn't remember not being on this conference call, which sounded more like a numbers station than a business meeting at this point.

The stench of cigarettes got a little less stale and some caterwauling slipped into the living room through the cracks in my bedroom door. I put the phone down on a mint-in-box exercise bike I'd bought when the outbreak had briefly made me more ambitious than agoraphobic. I listened. The cat had been workshopping her message—much less indifference and a greater degree of incitement against the inevitable advent of the gas-mask gestapo. There was something much more sinister going on here, she explained. Apocalypse, from the Greek "revelation," was never intended to describe the end of the world. It is a description of the realization that time is finite. Once we know that, she reasoned, how can we let them keep taking it from us, one mandatory sick day at a time?

I shook my head and checked my pockets for beer money. Someone out in the hallway let out a fearsome, dry cough.

Standoff at Bay Ridge - Sunday, April 19th, 2020

The bathroom door trembles in its frame as my cat slams her body into it, repeatedly. A lamp breaks somewhere beyond the door and now things are really starting to get rowdy in my living room. My cat has invited her Facebook group over to protest my self-isolation, and they are occupying the rest of my apartment decked out in tactical gear. The acrid odor of burning synthetics pours in through the crack under the door as the protestors light a hand sanitizer-fueled PPE bonfire.

I'm starting to feel like David fucking Koresh—the misunderstood guy in the TV show, not the real-life monster. There is an easy way and a hard way. I make the responsible choice and order three more jigsaw puzzles. It is important to keep your mind engaged with things other than viral loads. Somebody on the conference call asks if I'm having connection problems. I ignore them.

Amazon is out of stock, just in general. I keep hitting refresh any-
way. As long as the pages keep reloading, there is hope. Whoever wrote these
shopping lists did an atrocious job of organizing them. There is no hierarchy
of urgency, and the opportunity cost is staggering.

I am somewhere outside of myself as my wretched hands claw my
wish list into the search bar through pangs of carpal tunnel. The mob outside
the bathroom is chanting, "No one is non-essential," in between fearsome,
dry coughs. My searches for medical masks, nitrile gloves, Spaghetti-Os, and
a Nintendo Switch are all coming back in a surge of 503 Service Unavailable
Errors in one tab after another and I realize Brooklyn's months-long DDoS
attack on the e-commerce establishment has finally overwhelmed the system.
Someone on the conference call says they're hearing an echo and asks every-
one to mute.

My hair is full of paint chips and splinters. The door is buckling. I
tear off a strip of cloth from my T-shirt and ransack the under-sink cabinet
for some isopropyl alcohol to soak it in—it's not an N95, but it's better than
nothing. It occurs to me that the virus has breached the apartment when the
triumphant whooping of the protestors outside is drowned out by the deafen-
ing jackhammer of suppressing fire from their AR-15s as they attempt to hold
the Invisible Enemy at bay.

It is very rare in your lifetime to know that you are using the wifi
somewhere for the last time as it is happening, but as the gunfire dies down
and the coughing resumes at a rapid crescendo, I am keenly aware that I
have reached the end of something, and that if it is to be followed by another
beginning, it will be in a terrifying and unrecognizable new world. There is a
break in the 503 Errors just long enough to get through to the comment box
on Amazon's contact us page. I take the opportunity to carve my final legacy
into the walls of Pompeii as dark clouds gather over Vesuvius in the distance:
*Thank you for your heroic service in these unprecedented times. What is your
return policy on fitness equipment?*

Ada and the Line

Photography by Conor Gannon

Words by Sara Dallmayr

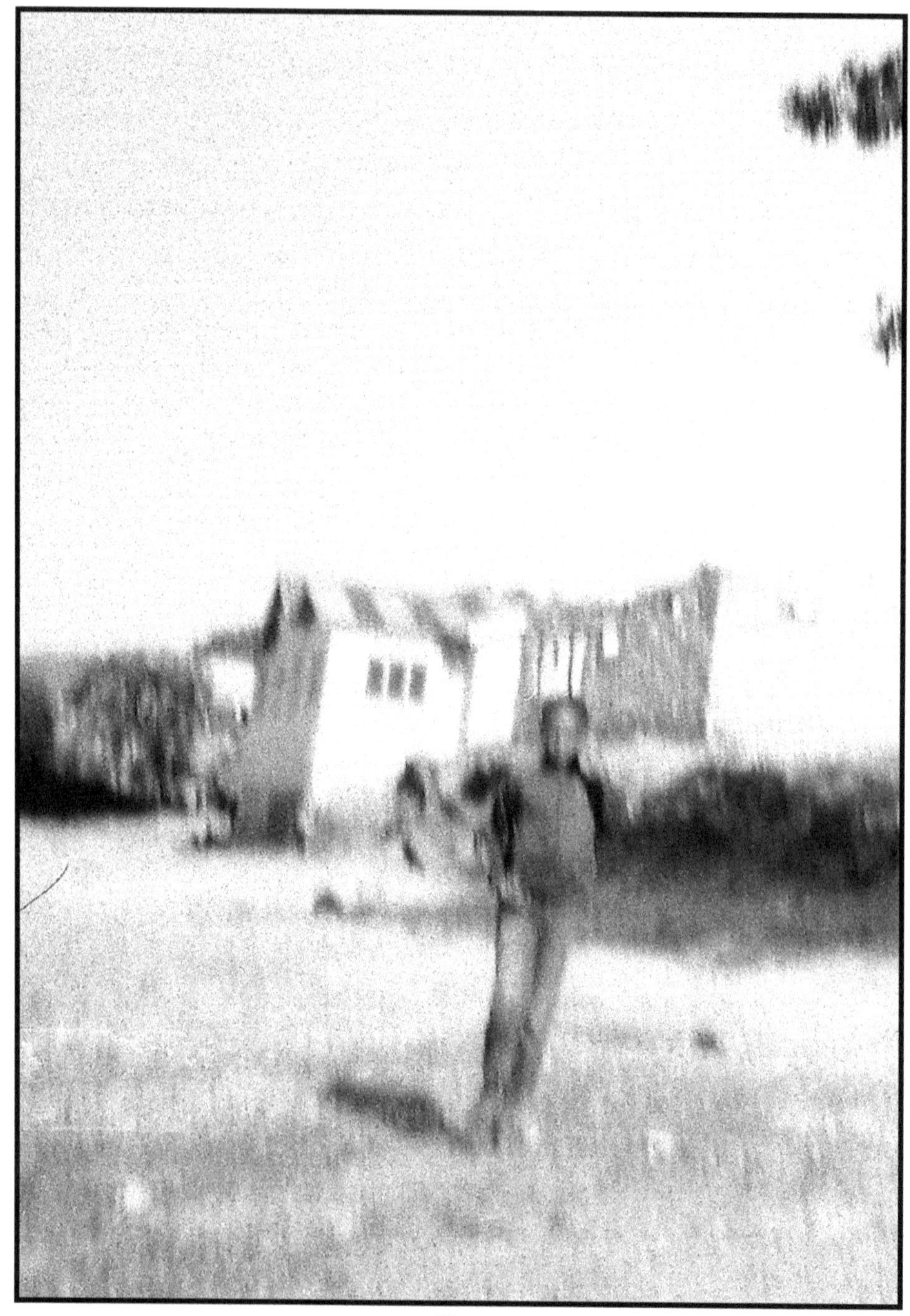

Looking back the crease began where we could all see it, drawn into the blanks of our insides, the bleak we could never see, the quiet world of trees and boats and growing things. The sky drank all the color of the day through its pale straw and spat it out into the next day's dawn. Every stone cast shade when we were children. The girl took one step forward because motion was a palm pressed upon her heart, and even today she moves like a fly so fast the paper can only chase it. Her memory berg underwater as she strikes the edge of your boat and throws every compass off kilter. Starboard, the house grows sideways. On the kitchen floor lies a tiled floor full of highway. A pane streaked with heat. Running up steps, out of breath.

In Order Of Appearance:

Caroline Rowe (née Zimmer) is a Pushcart Prize nominated poet and lifelong resident of the French Quarter in New Orleans. Her work has appeared in various publications including The Raw Art Review, Seems, Harbinger Asylum, and The Jabberwock Review, where she was a finalist for the Nancy D. Hargrove's Editor's Prize. She has also been anthologized in The Maple Leaf Rag (Portals Press.) Her debut chapbook, God's Favorite Redhead, is forthcoming from Lucky Bean Press.

Abe Winterscheidt is an author and photographer. As a photographer, he seeks to find beauty in nature and in the stars. Abe aims to photograph every protected site in the world. His gallery is available at www.imaginethesky.com. His instagram is @imaginetheskyphotography

James King is the recipient of the 2020 Academy of American Poets Prize from Dartmouth College. His work has appeared in the Stonefence Review, The Foundationalist, and forthcoming in Humana Obscura. When he is not writing, James enjoys reading comic books and baking homemade pizzas. He lives in Danville, NH, with his family and two dogs. Instagram handle: @jamn_king

Jason R. Montgomery, or JRM, is a Chicano/Indigenous Californian writer, painter, and playwright from El Centro, California. In 2016, along with Poet Alexandra Woolner, and illustrator Jen Wagner, JRM founded Attack Bear Press in Easthampton, MA. In 2019, JRM's art was featured at CreativeArts Workshop in New Haven, CT, and his solo show Aqui Y Alla at the MapSpace Gallery in Easthampton. JRM completed graduate studies at the University of California, Santa Barbara's Department of Theatre and Dance with an emphasis in Playwriting and Chicano Studies in 2006. JRM's work for the Coalescence show at Readywipe Gallery in January 2020 explored the cultural synthesis intrinsic to decolonization. Using found collage and construction materials, he merges Kumeyaay, Chumash, and Chicano designs and aesthetics to explore the history of US colonization, while synthesizing a decolonized motif that honors the complicated heritage of the postcolonial subject.
His work can be found at: www.attackbearpress.com Facebook: @attackbearpress
Instagram: @attackbearpress

Former Atlanta Youth Poet Laureate, Ninel Nekay is a Jamaican American southerner, writer, actress, and black mental health advocate. At age 15 she won her first poetry slam, shortly after Nekay also debuted in her first production at the Alliance theater. By 18 she became a 2-time nationally recognized writer and performer by way of Brave New Voices, one with over 6 awards under her belt. Before 21 Nekay had already performed at some of the country's most historically groundbreaking venues such as The Fox Theater, The Kennedy Center For The Performing Arts, The Center For Civil And Human Rights, The War Memorial Opera House, and more. In addition to her successes, organizations such as WE Day, Georgia Public Broadcasting, and The Alliance Theater contracted her in exchange for her services as a poetry and performance coach. Immensely grateful for her beginning in the arts as a youth, as an adult Nekay has refined her approach to the craft by utilizing her content as a method to educate onlookers with the intent to de-stigmatize mental health in the black community.

Lea Wülferth is a Brooklyn-based artist, exploring themes of freedom, identity, memory, and truth(s) on a personal and socio-political level across different media. She was named Author of the Month by Spillwords Press in December 2017 and has published poems and artwork in Chaleur Magazine, The Esthetic Apostle, Watershed Review and more. Her paintings and mixed media art have been exhibited at the A.I.R. Gallery, Brooklyn Museum, The Living Gallery and Pratt Institute, among other places. In 2017, she opened the YouTooCanWoo gallery in Brooklyn to provide opportunities to showcase and engage with the amazing artistic talent in her creative community and create immersive experiences. She graduated with master's degrees from the University of Oxford, England, and the Sorbonne in Paris, France. www.leawulferth.com @l_peregrine

Silja Cheong is a law and business student and writer living between Finland and China. Her poetry has previously been published in Into the Void and Hawai'i Review. ne.

Ma. Antonette Lofamia is a Filipino writer living in Japan. Published as Anya Lofamia, her works appear online and in print. Her work also appears in the recently published anthology in the Philippines, NARITO: Essays on Place. Currently, she is working on a poetry collection in completion of her MFA degree.

Joy Kloman earned her M.F.A. from the University of Florida and completed her B.F.A. at the Kansas City Art Institute. Her areas of emphasis were painting, printmaking, and drawing.
Kloman has taught students of all ages. Her experience includes teaching art at the University of Mississippi, Oxford, where she was a tenured associate professor of painting and drawing. She solely supervised the graduate and undergraduate painting program. Additionally, Kloman taught a drawing course in London, England.
Kloman was the recipient of a Mississippi Arts Commission Individual Artist State Grant. She has had work displayed in the The Drawing Center, Viewing Program & Slide Registry in New York. Furthermore, Kloman attended an artist residency in Hungary. One of her works is owned by Balatonfüred City Hall.
Her paintings and prints are in many public and private collections, including, but not limited to the Ringling Museum of Art, Florida, Gulf Coast Museum of Art, Pensacola Museum of Art, and the Meridian Museum of Art.

Stuart Terman is a physician, previously Assistant Clinical Professor/Ophthalmology/Case Western Reserve in his home city of Cleveland, married and blessed with 4 grown children. He's had publications in Medical/Literary/Surgical/Ocular Journals, including the 'Annals of Plastic Surgery', the 'Annals of Ophthalmology', the 'Consultant for Pediatricians', and 'The Ohio Family Physician' among a number of others. A picture he took last year was included in the High Shelf Press, Issue # 2 at https://www.highshelfpress.com/decembernewspaper.

Erin Block works as a librarian and freelance writer. She is the author of two books, The View from Coal Creek and By a Thread. Her work has been published in The Rumpus, The Columbia Review, Guernica and Gray's Sporting Journal, among others. She lives in a cabin in the Rocky Mountains of Colorado where she hunts, fishes, forages, and gardens.

Marj Hogan is a Spanish teacher living in Portland, Oregon. Her poems have been published in _The Rendezvous Reader: Northwest Writing_, the Cambridge, Massachusetts _New Voices_ series, the _Charles River Journal_, _Bear Deluxe_ magazine, and _VoiceCatcher_

Anna Genevieve Winham writes at the crossroads of science and the sublime, cyborgs and the surreal. She is Ninth Letter's 2020 literary award winner in Literary Nonfiction and Writer Advice Flash Fiction Contest's 2020 3rd place winner. Anna reads prose for Passengers Journal, and she writes and performs with the Poetry Society of New York. You can find her poetry in Q/A Poetry, Panoplyzine, Meniscus, Breadcrumbs Magazine, and others. Her prose appears or is forthcoming in Tilde~, Oxford Public Philosophy, Rock & Sling, Paragraph, Gold Man Review, and Passengers Journal. While attending Dartmouth College (which was the pits), she won the Stanley Prize for experimental essay and the Kaminsky Family Fund Award.

Andrea Jones lives in Liverpool, England and for the last nine years has taught art in prison.
Andrea has had her artwork published in Pikchur Magazine, Average Art magazine, Wotisart Magazine, Candy Floss magazine, Thought Art Magazine, Envision Arts Magazine and Art Hole Magazine.
She has exhibited her artwork in galleries and as part of The Beatles exhibition in Liverpool.
Andrea was commissioned by Go Penguins to be a part of an art trail in Liverpool. The artwork featured on the front cover of Go Penguins Souvenir Guide which sold in Tate Liverpool and featured in newspapers in India and Toronto.
Andrea also works as a promotional photographer for City Entertainment Group which is a theatre company based in Liverpool.
https://www.instagram.com/andrea_jones_art/
www.modandart.co.uk

Ellie Lynch is a junior at the University of Georgia studying English and Media.
Instagram: @e1ynch Twitter: @igucssellie

Claire Franken is a recent graduate of the University of Pittsburgh where she studied sociology, urban studies, and English nonfiction writing. She spent 10 months in Togo, West Africa as a health volunteer with the Peace Corps before being evacuated due to the global pandemic. Her work has never been published.

LAURIE ROSENWALD is a painter, author, humorist, and principal of rosenworld, a design, illustration and animation studio. Actually there is no studio, Miss Rosenwald usually works alone, and rosenworld doesn't exist. In spite of this, rosenworld.com was launched in 1995. Laurie also does humor writing, and writing which is only marginally funny. She's done many, many drawings for The New Yorker magazine, The New York Times, and other fine publications. She collaborated with author David Sedaris on a hilarious app, "David's Diary. Her most recent book is titled "all the wrong people have self-esteem" and is published by Bloomsbury. It is an inappropriate book for young ladies, and frankly, anybody else. Her New York Notebook is on sale at the George Pompidou Center in Paris, and her children's book, And To Name But Just a Few: Red, Yellow, Green, Blue was named a Scholastic Parent & Child Best Book. It is the only book your family will ever need.
-Laurie has had solo painting exhibitions at SPRING/BREAK ART FAIR 2020, curated by JOHN CHEIM, Galerie Pixi in Paris, among others. She paints with hot, colored wax. In other words, encaustic- a sadly misunderstood medium, much misused by hobbyists and amateurs- anyone who enjoys the smell of burning flesh. She divides her time between New York and Sweden, because she wants to have her cake, eat it too, and then she wants more cake. She speaks Swedish like a native New Yorker, and appeared as "Woman" on "The Sopranos," a role she was born to play. She can draw circles around other people that can draw circles, and claims to have won all the usual awards.

Sean Gallagher graduated from Wabash College with a bachelor's degree in English and from the University of Southern California with a master's degree in Journalism. Mr. Gallagher was a crime reporter in Hong Kong and now resides in Charleston, SC, working as a graphic designer/illustrator. His art was recently featured in Ariel's Dream Literary Journal.

Angus McLinn is a Brooklyn-based writer from the Upper Midwest. His award-winning short fiction has been anthologized in Writers Digest's 17th Annual Short Short Fiction Competition Collection, Songs of my Selfie: An Anthology of Millennial Stories, and the 2013 Saint Paul Almanac. His other poetry and fiction has also appeared in various literary journals in the US and abroad including Antithesis, The Other Stories, Blue Monday Review, and elsewhere.

Conor Gannon is a reluctant poet and mystic traversing material minefields of euphoria.

Sara Dallmayr is originally from Kalamazoo, Michigan. She received a BA in English from Western Michigan University. Dallmayr is currently a rural mail carrier in South Bend, Indiana. She lives with her husband and cats. Her work has appeared or is forthcoming in Third Coast, 3Elements, Eclectica, Texas Review, High Shelf Press, and others. Her hobbies include washing pet rocks and bass guitar.

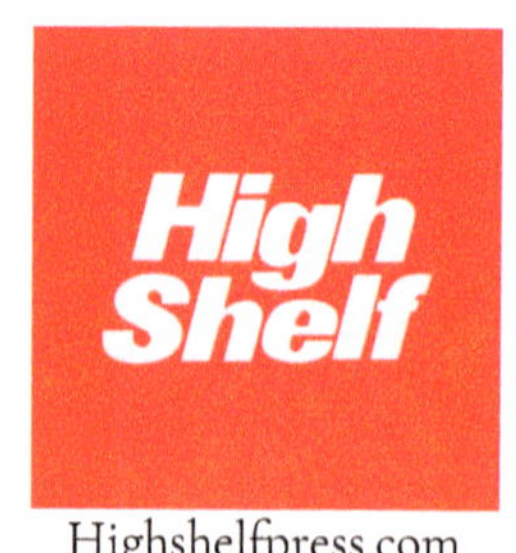

Highshelfpress.com